Can We Eat The Art?

Incredible Edibles and Art You *Can't* Eat

by Paula Guhin

Incentive Publications, Inc.
Nashville, Tennessee

This book is affectionately dedicated to two men in my life:
To my husband, who has the soul of an artist and who,
thankfully, shares my love of food, and to Cal Schultz, the
artist, art teacher, and dad I look up to.

Illustrated by David Schimmell
Cover by David Schimmell
Edited by Angela L. Reiner

Library of Congress Card Number: 0C-111248
ISBN 0-86530-471-8

PRINTED IN THE UNITED STATES OF AMERICA
www.incentivepublications.com

MENU
(Contents)

Introduction 6
Safety First 9
Author's Note 9
Supplies and Equipment 10

Part 1, Incredible Edibles

Pudding Painting 12
Bread Painting and Buttermilk Art 15
Play Clay You Can Eat 16
Sweet Tooth Sculpture 19
Spud Buddies and Food Friends 21
Faux Fabergé 23
Pretzel People and Salty Dogs 27
Painted Pumpkins and Gorgeous Gourds 29
Ever-Popular Popcorn 31
Dented Cans—Delightful! 33
Á La Carte Art: Snack Attack Still Life 36
Divide and Conquer: A Cross-Section Drawing 39

Part 2, Art You Can't Eat

Make Color Magic 42
Savor the Senses 44
One-Color Collage 46
Printmaking with Produce 47
Bird Food Fun 50
Sandpainting with Salt 51
Funny Foods (Illustrating Idioms) 53
Creative Kitchen Clays 54
Remarkable Recipes for Paint and Paste 58
Fantasy Food Faces 60
Hoagies and Heroes 64
Pasta Pictures, Noodle Jewels, & Bean Balls 65
Beautiful Breakfast—A Feast for the Eyes 70
Fun Batik with Flour 72
Great Granny Apples 74
Clay Food Creations 75
List of Lessons by Art Media 76
Glossary 77

Introduction

The idea of food as art is not new. Artists have used food as their subject for hundreds of years. Even the idea of art made from food is not new. Caterers serving fancy foods make them as aesthetically pleasing as possible by varying the colors and textures that make the meal. In the time-honored Japanese tea ceremony, there is beauty in the serving pieces and in the ritual itself.

Pop art, an art movement popular in the early 1960's, often used images borrowed from mass media sources. Andy Warhol, an American Pop artist, produced the well-known series of Campbell's Soup cans in 1962. Claes Oldenburg, a Swedish-born Chicagoan and Pop sculptor, often used foods as his subject: desserts, sandwiches, and more! In 1961, he wrote "I am for Kool-Art, 7-Up Art, Pepsi Art, Sunkist Art . . ."

Foods come in such a huge variety of wonderful shapes and colors! Is it any wonder they have inspired artists? Paintings and other art forms often have fruit bowls and dining-table fare as their subject. In 1963, Marcel Broodthaers began to produce works of art with mussel shells, representing a popular dish of his native Belgium. Wayne Thiebaud, an American artist, has done many still-life paintings of cafeteria goodies and bake shop specials. He used hot dogs, sandwiches, cakes, pies, and ice cream as his subjects in the early sixties. Fairly recently, sculptures have been made of butter, lard, and chocolate!

> *Please note: We are very aware that it would be inappropriate to use edibles as art supplies in settings where food is not plentiful. We are mindful that this is an area of sensitivity, and we urge you to examine your feelings concerning this matter.*

This book contains a wealth of projects that use foodstuffs and their containers in all sorts of artistic ways. Fruits and veggies gain personalities. Aluminum cans are transformed into sculptures. "Fabergé" eggs are enjoyable for artists of all ages. On the menu are recipes for fun that are tried 'n' true—a savory selection of how-to's. Just start from scratch and follow the step-by-step instructions, or "have it your way!" You might make adjustments to suit yourself and the needs of your students. Variations may be desirable or necessary.

Within the pages of **Can We Eat the Art?** you'll find a list of materials to "stock the larder." Many of the ingredients are inexpensive and are readily available at a grocery store. You will also find a glossary of terms and their definitions in the back of the book. On page 76, you will find a *List of Lessons According to Art Media*: acrylic paints, ceramic clay, fibers, watercolors, and more.

We have included suggested skills ratings:
- "It's Alimentary" (for Pre-K to Grade 2),
- "Intermediate Cuisine" (Grades 3 to 5), and
- "Advanced Gourmet" (Grades 6 to 8).

These age recommendations are intended to provide a general guide for you. **Can We Eat the Art?** is really for all ages and all stages.

A hand icon accompanies activities with which a helping hand is needed for younger children.

Another specialty of the house is the notation on estimated time needed to complete an activity:
- "Minutes in the Making,"
- "Done in an Hour," or
- "Best Finished Later."

(These guidelines are an approximation.)

We have used both two- and three-dimensional activities that have been kid-tested for success. The art experience is often accompanied by a "Side Dish," which provides a variation or alternative activity.

The projects here can and should be adapted for maximum originality. **Can We Eat the Art?** gives choices, and it leaves some of the decisions up to you.

The "Teacher's Tip" sections provide supplemental ideas related to other disciplines or curricula, practical suggestions, and interesting anecdotes to inspire student interest.

We have noted when an activity uses recycling *(Artful Use of Leftovers)* and when it is an *Easy Cleanup!* project.

We also present *Food for Thought*—which provides pointers on evaluating the finished artwork.

Can We Eat the Art? is divided into two sections.

Part 1: Incredible Edibles contains many instances when you might actually snack on your art materials! If "the proof is in the pudding," this is ample proof: You can have your fun and eat it too! Some of the finished art works in this section are meant to be admired (not consumed), but eating is definitely involved!

Part 2: Art You Can't Eat contains activities that may be at the height of good taste—but don't taste them! For example, the kitchen clays listed in Part 2 aren't very palatable, while you *can* and *will* want to eat the play clays in Part 1. The projects in each part generally become more advanced toward the end of each section.

Remember to take allergies and parental objections into consideration before dispensing edibles to children.

There are many experiences here to whet your appetite, and they are suitable for diverse ages and abilities. Discover "delicious" works of art to be created with common kitchen staples—a smorgasbord of budget-minded ideas. Holiday and seasonal experiences are included, and historical and cultural references are made. We hope you will turn to **Can We Eat the Art?** whenever you want to dish up some fun!

SAFETY FIRST

Most of the tools and materials called for in this book are safe. However, there are a few items which must be handled with extra caution. Adult supervision is necessary for several of the projects. Adult supervision is especially important when working at the kitchen stove.

Hand mixers require watchfulness when youngsters are using them.

Craft knives and paring knives are potentially dangerous, as are cut up aluminum cans. Handle all sharp objects with extreme care.

Low-temperature glue guns are available for your protection. If a hot glue gun is used, it is especially important to be vigilant. Serious burns have been sustained using such tools.

Spray varnishes or fixatives should be used with responsibility. Do not inhale the mist; use good ventilation. Vapors from permanent markers can also be harmful; use water-based markers instead.

Sewing needles are not for the negligent, and even such innocuous items as toothpicks are a concern when in the hands of young children.

Always remember to take food allergies into consideration.

Be wary, be careful, be safe!

AUTHOR'S NOTE

Art, like cooking, is a labor of love. I hope you'll consider this book "brain food." Take the listed ingredients—a dash of this, a pinch of that—and "soup them up" any way you please. Toss the ideas around, let them simmer, and then formulate your own recipes for success in art.

Made a mistake with one of the art experiences? Don't let it "eat" at you! If a recipe fails to satisfy, please don't "stew" over it. Experiment, explore, and try new directions and different approaches. Go for it with gusto!

Please display everyone's creations, taking turns if space is a problem. Celebrate and enjoy each child's unique approach.

It is my hope that **Can We Eat the Art?** will help the reader bring in a harvest of the imagination. Bon appétit.

Supplies and Equipment
(Everything you'll need from soup to nuts!)

Acrylic Paints
Alum
Aluminum Foil
Animal Crackers
Baking Soda
Blindfold
Bread
Breakfast Cereals
Cardboard or Matboard
Chalk Pastels
Charcoal
Cheese Spread
Clay, Glaze, and a Kiln
Coffee Filters
Colored Pencils
Construction Paper
Containers
Cookie Cutters
Cookie Dough
Cookie Sheet
Cooking Oil
Cornstarch
Corn Syrup
Cotton Batting
Craft Knife or Paring Knife
Cream of Tartar
Dried Beans
Eggs
Evaporated Milk or Buttermilk
Felt and Fabric Scraps
Fish
Fishing Line
Fixative
Flour
Food Coloring
Fruits and Vegetables
Glitter

Gloss Medium
Glue
Glue-Gun, Low Temperature
Gumdrops and Other Candies
Hammer
Hand Mixer
Honey or Light Corn Syrup
Ink
Instant Potatoes
Kitchen Flavorings and Powders
Kitchen utensils
Lemon Juice
Magazines
Markers
Marshmallows
Masking Tape
Measuring Cups and Spoons
Milk
Muslin
Newspapers
Oil Pastels
oven and Oven Mitts
Paint Brushes, Assorted
Paint Shirt or Smock
Paper
Paper Plates
Paper Towels
Pasta, Uncooked
Pastry Brush
Peanut Butter, Creamy
Peas
Pencils and Erasers
Pins, Round-headed and Pin
Findings
Plastic Squeeze Bottle
Pop cans
Pots and Pans

Powdered Drink Mix
Powdered Mix
Powdered Sugar
Pretzels
Pudding Mix
Raisins
Ribbon
Rice
Rolling Pin
Salt and Pepper
Saucepan
Scissors
Seeds
Sequins
Sewing Needles
Shelf Paper
Sieve
Small Bottle Caps or Lids
Snack Items
Sponge
Spoons
Spray Varnish
Strainer
Sugar, Crystal and Cubes
Tagboard or Bristol Board
Tempera Paint
Tennis Balls
Tissue
Toaster
Toothpicks
Vinegar
Wallpaper Sample Books
Watercolor Paints
Wax Crayons
Waxed Paper
Yarn

PART I
Incredible Edibles

"Art feeds the soul!"

With the projects in this section, you may take that sentence literally.

Some of the media in Part 1 are so tempting you just might succumb to the surge to eat your art! Pudding, pretzels, and popcorn are very appealing art materials. The baking potato used on page 21 can be "de-frocked" for dinner. Painted pumpkins can be baked later, too.

These art experiences are enough to "make your mouth water"—indulge!

When you see this sign, it means youngsters need a helping hand.

Pudding Painting

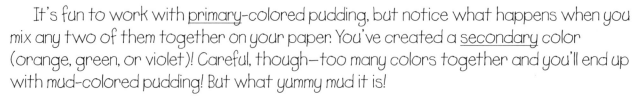
- It's Alimentary
- Minutes in the Making

You can make many colors of edible "fingerpaint" with just a few bottles of food coloring and some vanilla instant pudding. Along with red, yellow, and blue food coloring (and the pudding), you'll need:

- white shelf paper

- newspapers to cover the work space

- mixing bowls

- 2 cups cold milk, mixed with pudding according to directions

- electric mixer, used with adult supervision

It's fun to work with <u>primary</u>-colored pudding, but notice what happens when you mix any two of them together on your paper. You've created a <u>secondary</u> color (orange, green, or violet)! Careful, though—too many colors together and you'll end up with mud-colored pudding! But what yummy mud it is!

Use the side of your hand, the heel of your hand, and your knuckles. Try two or three fingers at a time, and use your fingernails, too.

Don't use just your hands! Drag tools through the colors: forks, potato mashers, spatulas—use your imagination!

You'll be consumed by creativity, and so will your "paint."

Cooked 'n' Colored Cornstarch

- It's Alimentary
- Minutes in the Making

This homemade finger paint may not be as tasty as the pudding variety, but it's almost as easy. This method was once used to decorate papers for bookbinding.

Mix $\frac{1}{4}$ cup cornstarch with 2 cups cold water. Bring to a boil on the stove (with adult supervision). Let cool, then pour into containers. Add food coloring and mix well.

When you're ready to use the mixture, brush your starch paint onto paper and scrape tools across the paint to form designs. Use texturing tools such as combs, toothpicks, or cardboard with notches cut into the edge.

Pink Ink And More—It's Berry Fun!

- Alimentary to Intermediate Cuisine
- Minutes in the Making

While these recipes are not for fingerpaint, they are dist-ink-tive, nonetheless!

You can make your own ink from the juice of cherries, blackberries, strawberries, blueberries, and raspberries. Push the berries through a sieve which you have placed over a bowl to collect the juice.

Add $\frac{1}{2}$ teaspoon salt and $\frac{1}{2}$ teaspoon vinegar to the juice. Use a dip pen or a brush to write or draw with your ink. Be careful to protect your clothes by wearing a smock!

Store the mixture in a lidded container that has been marked "NOT FOR DRINKING." Make some ink-credible colored inks soon! Try other kinds of fruits to see what colors you can make!

Teacher's Tip

It is believed the Chinese discovered ink nearly 4,500 years ago. They mixed lamp black and a glue with water. Such inks are still used today! They are called India inks and are quite permanent.

Natural Dyes

- Alimentary to Intermediate Cuisine
- Done in an Hour

You can use materials from nature to create dyes at the stove. You'll need an enamel or glass pot with a lid, some lidded storage containers, water (distilled or rainwater is best), spoons, a large bowl, and a colander or strainer. (Alum is optional.)

Choose from spinach (for green dye), red onion skins (for a reddish-brown), cut-up beets (magenta), walnut shells (brown), and cranberries (red). Cover with water in the pot and bring to a boil. Reduce heat and simmer for about 45 minutes, stirring occasionally. Remove from heat and cool. Strain over bowl. Add a teaspoon of alum to the mixture to set the dye, if desired. Pour dye into glass storage containers. (You can also achieve a rich brown dye by an easier method: Dissolve instant coffee in hot water!)

Wearing an apron or a smock, you can use your homemade dye to color white yarn or fabric. Make sure the fibers are not synthetic—use wool yarn or cotton cloth.

Kool-Aid Dye

- Alimentary to Intermediate Cuisine
- Done in an Hour

Use powdered drink mixes in beautiful colors to make your own dyes. You'll need two packages of the unsweetened mix, a lidded cooking pot, white vinegar, a stove, water, and lidded storage containers.

Pour the dry mixes into the pot, add $1/2$ cup vinegar and $1/2$ gallon water. Heat to boiling (with adult supervision, of course). Simmer for 20 minutes. Cool and pour into containers.

Try tie-dyeing a white T-shirt with this dye, or paint the dye on a T-shirt with a brush or Q-tip.

Bread Painting and Buttermilk Art

Bread Painting

- It's Alimentary
- Minutes in the Making
- Easy Clean Up!

Painted toast is pretty and practical—you can eat your canvas now or later!

Gather together the following: slices of white bread, milk, food coloring, containers, new paintbrushes, and a toaster.

Put several tablespoons of milk into each of four or more containers. Add a few drops of food coloring to the milk in each container. Use a clean, new paintbrush to apply your milk paint to the bread in the design of your choice. Be careful not to soak the bread. When your design is finished, toast the bread lightly. The paintings may be frozen for later use. (If you freeze them, be sure to wrap them well first.)

Be the "toast of the town" with this idea!

Teacher's Tip

- For teachers of toddlers, there's a playful rhyme available on tape called "Peanut Butter and Jelly," from Puffin Story Tapes.

- Use bread to involve older students in a science project: Grow mold! Explain that many of the tiny pieces of dust in the air are fungus spores, or tiny plants that will start to grow if they fall on the right piece of food! Put a slice of bread on a plate and sprinkle it with water. Rub a finger on a dusty window sill to pick up spores, and then rub the dust on the bread. Next, put the plate in a plastic bag and twist the bag shut. Put it in a warm place and look at it each day with a magnifying glass. Eventually you'll see tiny threads of mold branching across the surface.

Buttermilk Art

- Alimentary to Intermediate Cuisine
- Done in an Hour

Kids love colored chalk, but the art is dusty and matte. With this method, the work will have a gorgeous glossy effect when dry!

Along with the colored chalk and buttermilk (or evaporated milk), you'll need a paintbrush and white drawing paper.

Paint a thin coat of buttermilk over the paper, and draw into it with colored chalks while it is still wet.

Play Clay You Can Eat

- It's Alimentary
- Done in an Hour

Have a craving to get your hands on some clay? You can create and eat to your heart's content with these culinary clays. Both recipes have something in common—peanut butter.

Delicious Modeling Clay

- $2/3$ cup creamy peanut butter
- $2/3$ cup honey
- 2 cups instant powdered milk

Mix all the ingredients together well. Then, with clean hands, form the clay into figures, animals, or other small sculptures. Then dig in and gobble 'em up!

Edible Play Dough

- 1 cup creamy peanut butter
- 1 cup light corn syrup
- $1^1/_2$ cups powdered milk
- $1^1/_2$ cups powdered sugar

Combine all the ingredients, beating until smooth. Refrigerate for several hours if a stiffer consistency is desired. Then make scrumptious sculptures!

Stained Glass Cookies

- Intermediate Cuisine to Advanced Gourmet
- Minutes in the Making

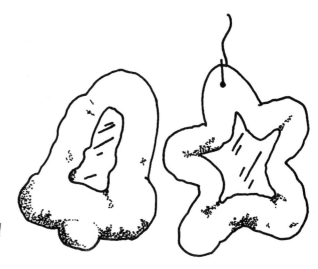

Many cathedrals all over the world have beautiful stained glass windows—colored glass panes held in place with lead. You can make "stained glass" cookies that can be hung in windows for the light to pass through your "panes." Or, you can eat them!

You'll need:

- refrigerated cookie dough
- assorted colors of hard candies (Lifesavers, sour balls, even sugar-free hard candies!)
- oven and oven mitt or hot pad

- hammer
- waxed paper
- aluminum foil
- cookie sheet

Chill the dough thoroughly. On waxed paper, roll it out into "ropes" no thicker than a pencil. Then, on aluminum foil, arrange the ropes of dough into shapes with "windows," or openings. For example, you could make a butterfly with spaces in its wings. Chanukah designs could include a Star of David or a dreidel. Christmas designs could include a bell shape or a Christmas tree. You might even try to make a church window! Make the openings big enough inside the shapes—the dough will spread later and partially fill the spaces. Be sure the enclosed spaces are well-sealed at the ends, too (so the candy won't leak out when it melts).

Next, place your creation on a cookie sheet, foil and all. Bake your designs at 350 degrees for five minutes only, and then remove from the oven. This pre-baking may leave the cookies lightly golden in color, not brown. If you wish to make a hole at the cookies' tops (so you can hang them up later), do so now.

Fill the open sections with crushed candy that you have broken up with a hammer (wrap the candies in waxed paper before breaking them). If you have large open spaces, you may use whole candies. The candy layer should be just as deep as the thickness of the dough. If you mix candy colors in one space, the color variations may become very pretty or not, depending on whether you use color "opposites." Avoid red and green together in one space, as well as yellow and purple, or blue and orange. Those pairs, when blended, become brownish or gray.

Return the cookies to the oven for about three minutes, or until the candy has melted. Remove from the oven and cool completely before carefully peeling the foil from the back of each cookie.

Teacher's Tip

An alternate event, using ready-made cookies, is a COOKIE-DECORATING CONTEST! With all the great trimmings and toppings available in the grocery stores today, it would be lots of fun. Parental help with this one is invaluable (and watch dietary restrictions).

Assemble glossy gels in squeeze tubes, candy snowflakes, nonpareils, colored sugar granules, pastel wafers, M & M's, gumdrops, colored sprinkles, red hots, nuts, licorice whips, miniature marshmallows, coconut, color shots, and cake decorations on cards. Thinned icing can be painted onto cookies with brand-new clean paintbrushes.

Before the tasty art works are consumed, they must be admired. You might have categories in your contest ("most colorful," "most humorous," and "most-of-everything"). Everybody wins!

Edible Potato Sculpture

- It's Alimentary
- Done in an Hour

"Smashed" potato sculptures are instant fun! You'll need:

- instant mashed potatoes, prepared according to directions
- two eggs, separated
- baking dish, buttered
- pastry brush
- modeling tools such as toothpicks, spoons, Popsicle™ sticks

Beat two egg yolks into the potato mixture. Then form sculptures such as animals, human heads, things found in nature—use your imagination! Place the sculptures into the greased baking dish. Beat two egg whites and brush onto the sculptures. Bake in an oven at 350 degrees until lightly browned. Allow to cool somewhat before serving.

> **"K**eep your words soft and sweet.
> You never know when you'll have to eat them."
>
> Unknown

Sweet Tooth Sculpture

- Alimentary to Intermediate Cuisine
- Minutes in the Making
- Perfect for Partners

"How Sweet It Is!"

Use two simple "construction" materials to build fantastic structures—it's fast, fun, and easy! Toothpicks (round or flat) serve as your construction beams. Gumdrops (ju-jus, spice drops), raisins, jelly beans, or marshmallows suffice as your connectors. If you use marshmallows, choose the miniature size.

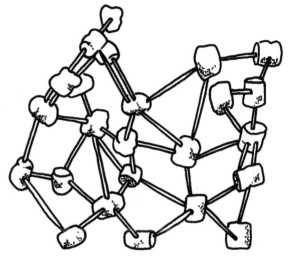

As you work on your assemblage, remember that triangular shapes form the strongest, most stable structure. Work "in the round," turning your piece as you progress. You may cut or break toothpicks into shorter lengths if desired. Try geodesic domes, towers, or robots! Have a contest in which the sturdiest and the tallest sculptures win. Participants might be cautioned to not eat their building materials until after the competition!

For variety, combine both sizes of marshmallows (regular-sized and small) or use colored toothpicks instead of plain. You can even use thin pretzel sticks instead of toothpicks.

If you can resist de-constructing and devouring your sculpture, it will harden in a few days and become stronger.

Food For Thought

 A stabile is an unmoving sculpture which can be viewed from all sides ("in the round"). An assemblage is an additive sculpture method, because the artist adds together the materials.

1. Is your sculpture well-balanced? Is it interesting from all sides?

2. Is it wobbly, or does it seem sturdy and well-crafted?

Teacher's Tip

- These sweet assemblages make a great science project for the study of crystals. If using miniature marshmallows, spread them on a cookie sheet and let them harden overnight before you build "crystals." Research the structure of the model you choose to build: square pyramid, tetrahedron, hexahedron, octahedron, etc. "Building" these forms with a computer program is another option.

- Raisins were mentioned on page 10 as a possible building material. Another science project to try is to make raisins dance! It's a magical phenomenon, lasting about an hour or more, and all you need is a pint jar, water, raisins, vinegar, and soda! Fill the jar with water and add several tablespoons of vinegar. Also add several raisins and a tablespoon of soda. No need to stir. Bubbles of carbon dioxide (formed by mixing the soda with an acid) attach themselves to the raisins, lifting them to the surface of the water. As the bubbles pop, the raisins sink.

Sugar Cube Igloo

- Intermediate Cuisine
- Best Finished Later

Start with a base row of sugar cubes around a cardboard circle cut to be about 7 inches in diameter. Leave a space for the entrance. Mix up a "mortar" to adhere the next layer of cubes: Add 2 egg whites to 3 cups of powdered sugar. Apply the "mortar" to the bottom of the added cubes (not to the tops of those already in place). Stagger the cubes as bricklayers do. Decrease the circumference gradually as you add each layer. After about 5 layers you might stop and let the igloo dry overnight. Then add about 4 more layers and the roof. Create the roof separately, on a flat surface, and when the mortar is dry you can place it on top. An arch for the entrance may be made the same way. Then sprinkle sugar snowdrifts around your winter abode.

If you're studying the Middle Ages, use the same technique to build a sugar cube castle and battlements!

Cheese Spread Cement—Building a Construction

- Intermediate Cuisine
- Done in an Hour

The variety of snack foods available today is mind-boggling! Instead of sweet stuff, "building materials" could include bread sticks, corn chips, onion rings, and cheese curls. Try using cheese spread to glue a construction together. You'll need a knife to spread the "cement," and paper plates to hold your snack foods. Try a mix of sturdy items like pretzels or crackers with such decorative snacks as popcorn or potato chips.

Spud Buddies and Food Friends

- Alimentary to Intermediate Cuisine
- Artful Use of Leftovers
- Done in an Hour

Don't stop with making just the mister potato. How about a potato-head wife or a baby potato-head? Create the whole family!

Assemble large scrubbed potatoes, toothpicks, construction paper, felt scraps and play-dough. Use the play-dough to make noses, lips, and ears, and affix them to the potatoes with short pieces of toothpick. Eyes can be cut from colored paper or felt, as can beards and moustaches. Pipe cleaners make great eyeglasses. Curl paper, or use yarn or an old scrubber pad for hair!

Use up-ended paper cups with the bottoms cut out as holders for your heads. Decorate these "necks" with ribbons, drawn-on collars, or bow ties. Potato people are nifty-looking and nutritious!

Your food friends can be completely edible if you use goodies for the decorations. Turn fruits or vegetables into funny faces or crazy creatures that you can eat all up!

Make a silly animal or person from a pear, peach, apple, banana, cucumber, orange, lemon, or plum. For facial features, arms, and legs, use grapes, cherries, raisins, marshmallows, apple slices, olives, celery, cloves, radishes, mushrooms, cubed potatoes, or chunks of cheese. Try popcorn hair, pretzel ears, and peanuts (in the shell) for a nose. Use toothpicks to fasten the foods together.

Instead of funny characters, another option is to make veggie vehicles like cars or planes.

Think of an original name for your creation. If you can bear it, eat what you've made. (Be sure to remove all the toothpicks first!)

Teacher's Tip

- After the fruit and vegetable critters are done, ask your students to write an imaginative story about their character.

- Studying the 19th century? You can make an edible "log cabin". Use carrot or celery sticks notched with a paring knife. "Chink" the spaces with cream cheese. Make a cardboard roof and shingle it with Triscuit cracker "shakes." Use egg white or flour paste as glue. Build the chimney with caramel "bricks" and peanut butter.

- How about a science experiment with a celery stalk? Place the celery in an empty water glass and it will be limp and droopy the next day. When you later place water in the glass, the stalk will eventually stand up straight again! Discuss osmosis and point out that the spots on a cut section of celery are the little tubes that carry fluids through the stalk.

"You can't make an omelette without breaking eggs."

Robespierre

Faux Fabergé

- Intermediate Cuisine
- Best Finished Later
- Artful Use of Leftovers

Jeweled, elegant, precious objects—eggs decorated with gold, diamonds, and more! Peter Carl Fabergé was a Russian goldsmith who created exquisite masterpieces in the late 1800's and early 1900's. His celebrated imperial eggs were the delight of royalty and the rich. He produced over fifty of these luxurious eggs, often including small surprises inside them.

You, too, can create "egg-citing" works, although your trimmings will be a bit more modest than rubies and gold! You'll need eggs, a needle, a bowl, watercolors, uncooked macaroni, and glue. You might also use glitter, sequins, ribbon, braid, and other similar decorations.

First, empty your egg. Use a needle to make a pinhole at each end of the uncooked egg. The bottom hole (at the large end of the egg) should be the biggest. Blow through the top hole, emptying the egg's contents into a bowl. (It helps if you've pierced the yolk with the needle.) Room temperature eggs are easier to blow. **NOTE: DO NOT SUCK IN!** Raw egg may contain bacteria.

If you plan to use the egg's contents to make an omelette or scrambled eggs, refrigerate the contents promptly and use them soon.

For strength, let the hollowed eggshell dry for a day before you decorate it. Next, use watercolors to paint uncooked macaroni in several "jewel-tones." Let dry. When the paint is dry, glue your macaroni baubles onto the egg. Nestle the pieces of pasta very close to each other, fitting them together like puzzle pieces. Add a coat of gloss medium for a shiny finish. Place on waxed paper to dry. When dry, you may add "egg-stra" embellishments such as gold braid. Stand your creation in a cup or a paper cuff used as a holder.

Other edibles can be substituted for painted macaroni to decorate the eggs. Color-coated candies are a beautiful alternative. You may also choose to go the natural route on white or brown eggs and use sunflower seeds, uncooked rice, dried beans, and split peas. Egg-straordinary!

Peter Carl Fabergé would be proud of you.

Marbleized Eggs

- It's Alimentary
- Minutes in the Making

For an incredibly fast and easy way to decorate eggs without all the gluing mentioned above, try this dyeing trick. You'll need food coloring, paper towels or napkins, aluminum foil, and hard-boiled eggs.

Place the paper towel or napkin on a sheet of foil. Put 8 to 10 drops of food coloring (use several different colors) near each other in the center of the paper towel or napkin. In a few moments the color will spread about 6" across. Place a damp egg in the center of the colored spot.

Starting underneath, gently press the foil snugly around the egg—paper towel and all. Work your way around to the top until the egg is completely wrapped. Soon you may carefully peel back the foil and paper towel together. Let the egg dry.

You can use one set of materials to color quite a few eggs. Once the paper napkin is saturated with damp color, you may use dry eggs. To keep the color from rubbing off onto hands or clothes, keep the finished eggs away from moisture.

Egg-cellent—it's marbleizing magic!

Teacher's Tip

- Almost every country in the world has some traditions concerning eggs. In feudal days, it was a custom for poor farmers (serfs) to give eggs to their landlords. This exchange of eggs represented new life each spring.

- A popular Greek tradition to try with hard-boiled eggs is to ask two kids to tap them together. The first to crack the other's eggshell is meant to have good luck!

- Germans colored eggs green on Holy Thursday and carried them for good luck. French brides of long ago broke an egg (also for luck) before entering the marriage house. An ancient Ukrainian legend tells of a dreadful creature bound in chains and waiting to destroy the earth. Each year its minions roam the world, counting the colorfully decorated eggs known as pysanky. If they find only a few, the beast's chains become looser. If they find many, its chains are made tight again.

- Try this science "magic" trick (it proves a floating object is less dense than the fluid it is floating in): First, hard-boil an egg and put it in a jar that is 3/4 full of water. The egg, heavier than the water, will sink to the bottom. Then remove the egg and add 3 teaspoons or more of salt to the water. This time the egg will float, since the heavier solution now supports the egg.

- You won't have egg on your face if you use this recycling tip: The old-style, molded-paper egg cartons are great for papermaking! Some of them are already colored, too. Just tear them up, soak the pieces in water, and blend with water in a blender. You've just made paper pulp. Pour through a screen, press out the excess water, and invert the pulp onto a Formica counter top. Shape, press, and let dry for your own egg-ceptional sheet of paper!

- There is a book which explains that many different creatures grow from eggs: "Chickens Aren't the Only Ones," by Ruth Heller (Grosset, 1981). Two books from Abrams Publishing are "Imperial Surprises" by Margaret Kelly, and "Carl Fabergé" by Gesa von Habsburg.

Answers for The Double Letters Game, page 26

These are just some of the foods with double letters in their names:

apples	cherries	pudding
beets	eggs	rolls
broccoli	herring	snapper
butter	lettuce	spaghetti
cabbage	mushrooms	strawberries
carrots	noodles	stuffing
cheese	pepperoni	waffles
	pizza	

The Double Letters Game

Many foods have double letters in their names. (Eggs and carrots are two examples.)
In the spaces below, name as many foods containing double letters as you can.

1. _____

2. _____

3. _____

4. _____

5. _____

6. _____

7. _____

8. _____

9. _____

10. _____

11. _____

12. _____

13. _____

14. _____

15. _____

16. _____

17. _____

18. _____

19. _____

20. _____

Pretzel People and Salty Dogs

- Intermediate Cuisine
- Done in an Hour
- Easy Clean Up!

"Crazy crullers," "crooked crumpets," "buckle biscuits"—crisp, crunchy morsels of salty goodness: pretzels! Brittle biscuits twisted like knots, and glazed and crusted with coarse salt, pretzels were invented by early Christians who were forbidden, during the Lenten fast, to use fat, eggs, or milk. To make bread without those products, they mixed a dough of flour, water, and salt. The result, shaped into two "arms" crossed in prayer, was called bracellae, which means "little arms." The name eventually became "pretzel."

For a drawing activity (a real treat!) based on these twisted biscuits, you'll need a bag of pretzels in the traditional knotted shape. You'll also need drawing tools such as pencils, crayons or markers, and 9" x 12" white drawing paper.

Go ahead and eat some of your pretzels, but keep one to observe closely. Study the familiar shape and then draw it in pencil on your white paper. Sketch lightly and large, adding the coarse salt "bumps" only if you wish.

Next, hold up your drawing and regard it from all four sides. What do you see there, besides a pretzel? With some imagination, could it be a racetrack? An insect? An alien or dog's head? Decide what you want to make from your drawing and add any details you wish. Erase any of the original lines you choose not to use. Soon the pretzel picture will be transformed! Finish with colored markers, crayons, or colored pencils.

Pretzel pictures are a playful and productive way to spend under an hour of your time. Use "pretzel power"—make your own "crazy cracker" creations!

Pretzels: What a Relief!

- Alimentary to Intermediate Cuisine
- Done in an Hour

They come in all shapes and sizes—from twists, sticks, nuggets, and knots all the way to goldfish! Use an assortment of pretzels to make a savory relief sculpture. Use your willpower to keep from consuming too much of your main art material as you complete your arrangement!

A "relief sculpture" is one that is slightly raised from a flat background; your pretzel pattern will project slightly from a flat surface. Choose a piece of cardboard or matboard in a color that looks good with the colors of the pretzels.

Next, pick a variety of pretzels to use—fat, thin, long, short—in several different shapes. Arrange them on your background very close to each other in some places and farther apart in others. When you're pleased with the way your design looks, glue the pretzel pieces down. **Hint: Rather than applying glue to each pretzel individually, you might spread an area of glue on your background and set the pretzels into the glue.**

Going Crackers

- It's Alimentary
- Done in an Hour

While animal crackers aren't exactly pretzels, they <u>can</u> be the basis of artwork.

The story of the Deluge and of Noah's Ark is a familiar one to many. There are similar ancient flood stories in the folklore of several different cultures. You can draw your own version of an ark on sturdy drawing paper or posterboard (12" x 18" or larger). Add scenery that includes land and rainwater. Use chalk, oil pastels, markers, or crayons to color it. Then, glue on animal crackers, two of each kind, and there you have it—a mixed-media marvel!

You can also cover animal crackers with three coats of clear acrylic, and (when dry) carefully use a glue gun to fasten on pin findings or button-cover backs.

While you certainly can munch a few crackers as you create these art works, the finished products are for viewing only.

Teacher's Tip

- Some feel the word "pretzel" is derived from the Latin <u>pretiola</u>, which means "small reward." In the old days pretzels were worn around the neck or hung on trees for good luck.

- Little pretzel wreaths are a holiday production that can hang on the tree. You'll need an 8-oz. bag of bite-sized pretzel twists to make about 10 wreaths. You also need waxed paper, glue, and ribbon for a bow. This wreath is not for consumption.

  Lay pretzels on the waxed paper in a circle, overlapping each other. Glue the layers together, let dry, remove from the waxed paper, and add a bow if desired.

Painted Pumpkins and Gorgeous Gourds

- Intermediate Cuisine to Advanced Gourmet
- Best Finished Later

These homemade holiday art works are better than any commercial decorations. They're loads of fun and practical, too—after Halloween the pumpkin contents can be scooped out and made into pies. Now <u>that's</u> creativity with cuisine!

Choose a pleasing, unblemished pumpkin that sits up nicely without toppling over. Use a black waterbased marker to outline expressive eyes, brows, nose, and mouth. You may wish to add drawn-on hair or lashes. Is your pumpkin-person sad? Add a big teardrop. Happy? Large round cheeks. Angry? Frown lines and marks from the nose to the corners of the down-turned mouth. If you make a mistake, simply wipe it off with a damp paper towel.

When you're ready to begin painting, wear a smock or a paint shirt. Use acrylics and good-quality brushes in several sizes, including a small, fine brush. To avoid smearing, let one area and color of paint dry before working right next to it with another color. Again, if mistakes are made, simply wipe off and start again.

As a finishing touch when you're done painting, you can outline all the shapes in permanent black marker to sharpen the edges. Finally, lightly spray with a protective coat of clear acrylic.

For even more fun, garnish your creation with a wig, an old hat, eyeglasses, or a yarn "moustache." Carefully use a glue gun, if necessary, to hold the accessories in place.

For an fun autumn alternative, try making a fantastic face on a golden gourd. It's as "easy as pie!"

Double Duty

- Intermediate Cuisine to Advanced Gourmet
- Best Finished Later

Sometimes two faces are better than one! Try one expression on one side of the pumpkin, and another emotion on the reverse. Your pumpkin will have a "split personality," happy and sad, or angry and surprised!

Another idea is to add a body. Stuff old clothes with crumpled newspapers and attach them to your pumpkin head. Pin the shirt to the pants and add old shoes and gloves.

Another Halloween Treat

- Intermediate Cuisine to Advanced Gourmet
- Done in an Hour

Instead of painting a face onto your pumpkin, you might adhere fruits or veggies with toothpicks. For example, cherries or grapes could be used for eyes, stringbeans for eyebrows or a mouth, a plum for the nose and orange sections for ears.

Teacher's Tip

- Halloween was probably first celebrated by Celts and Druids about 2,000 years ago. Then, about 1,000 years ago, the Catholic Church established All Saints Day, and the service on that day (November 1) was called "Allhallowmas." "All Hallow's Eve" on October 31 became what we call Halloween.

- The Pilgrims sometimes built scarecrows with pumpkin heads. Students can research pumpkins to find out how they are grown, whether they are a fruit or vegetable, and when the carving of jack-o'-lanterns began.

- Make "ghostly" favors for a class party by covering lollipops with white tissue and tying a piece of white thread under each sucker to secure the tissue. Another "fang-tastic" treat for Halloween parties (or a nutritious snack anytime) is roasted pumpkin seeds. Arrange the washed seeds on a cookie sheet, add a little oil, and place in the oven at 300 degrees until brown. As you munch these, read "The Little Old Lady Who Was Not Afraid of Anything" by Linda Williams (Crowell, 1986).

- Classroom cue: As students bring their pumpkins to school for painting, ask them to put their names on the bottoms with permanent ink, to avoid cases of "mistaken identity." Also, if the finished pumpkin people are to be displayed, let it be in a supervised area or a locked case.

Ever-Popular Popcorn

- Advanced Gourmet
- Done in an Hour

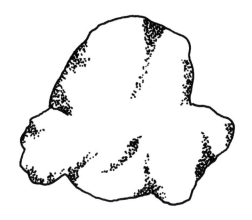

Plump kernels of popped corn can perform a double duty; they can be eaten as a yummy snack and they can be drawn as a study of form.

Find a fat, fluffy piece in your next bag or box of popcorn. Look at it very closely and find an interesting "view." Study the lines, shapes, and masses you see there. Scrutinize the light and dark areas and the textures.

On 9" x 12" white drawing paper, sketch lightly in pencil as you closely observe the object. Draw not only the outlines, but also the cracks, crevices, lumps, and bumps of the piece. Work large—work ten times as large as the original!

The forms will appear to take up more space (and look three-dimensional) if you use shading. Careful examination of your real-life piece will tell you which areas are highlighted and which are in shadow. Hold your pencil horizontally, with the "lead" flat to the paper, and shade the areas which should recede. You can soften the shading by using your fingertip and blending it toward the highlighted areas (which are left as clean, white paper).

To "ground" your form on the paper you can add a suggestion of cast shadow. In fact, if you investigate your real popcorn piece on the table-top, you'll probably see a real shadow underneath it.

Finally, add a few darkened contour lines to sharpen up the edges of your drawn object, and you're done! What a way to produce a delicious drawing! Go ahead and pore over some popcorn.

> **"P**art of the secret of success in life is to eat what you like and let the food fight it out inside."
>
> Mark Twain

Popcorn Form

Food For Thought

1. Does your drawing use a full range of values (lights and darks), or is it too pale?

2. Does the form appear rounded and three-dimensional instead of flat?

3. Does the form have some sharp outlines or is it too "fuzzy" around the edges?

4. Did you remember to cast a shadow on the ground?

Teacher's Tip

- Classroom hint: Providing a separate bag of popcorn for each student may be impractical . . . use paper cups full of popcorn and have a broom handy for the kernels that wind up on the floor!

- Here's a great cooperative game for younger children: Make popcorn the old-fashioned way! Pretend the floor is the hot part of a stove top. Have the kids crouch on the floor, and turn the "stove" on. As the floor heats up, the children begin to "pop" all over! They can pop all they wish, but when they've all become fluffy kernels, pour an imaginary sticky syrup all over them. As they touch each other they'll "stick" (hold hands) until they've formed a huge popcorn ball!

- An old American Indian legend says that a tiny spirit lived inside the popcorn kernel. When the corn popped it was because the spirit wanted to escape.

  Here's the scientific explanation: Heat makes the liquid inside a popcorn kernel turn into a gas. This gas takes up more room, so the pressure grows inside the kernel until the hard outer shell explodes and the starch from the inside comes to the outside. When popped, good popcorn expands over 30 times the size of the original kernel.

Dented Cans–Delightful!

- Advanced Gourmet
- Best Finished Later
- Easy Clean Up!

After you empty it, take a good look at that colorful soda pop can before you toss it into the recycling bin. See the light glint off a curve in the metal? Now squeeze a dent into the can and observe it again. Is there a shaded area in the "valley" you just made? "Hills" and "valleys," highlights and shadows: these are the makings of an interesting artwork based on the ever-popular pop can!

With close scrutiny and careful execution, you can create a realistic representation of a dented beverage container. Yes, you CAN!

Why dented? Because the depressions add texture, they add interest, and they create more values.

Ready? You'll need the slightly dented pop can, white drawing paper, pencil, eraser, and crayons. You may choose to use oil pastels, markers, or colored pencils instead of crayons.

Directions for Dented Cans—Delightful!

1. **FIRST,** decide which way you want your can to go—standing up or on its side?

2. **NEXT,** use your pencil to lightly sketch the can's contours (outlines) on your paper, a bit larger than life-size. Work vertically (up and down) on your paper if the can is standing upright, horizontally (across) if it's not.

3. **THEN,** after the outline is finished, look at the entire shape you've drawn. Are the proportions correct compared to the actual can? Does the height look right when compared to the width?

4. **NOW,** begin to sketch the contours of the dents. Follow the ridges and the dented-in shapes with your eyes. Pencil them in.

5. **FINALLY,** draw the details like rims, pull-tab, lettering, and patterns. Be careful to distort (twist and bend) lines and shapes wherever there's a dent. Letters will "wrap" around the forms, even disappearing in places! Draw them as you really see them, not as they looked before the denting took place.

6. **ADDING COLOR AND VALUES,** you might begin with a white crayon, heavily, wherever a strong highlight appears on the can. White crayon won't show on white paper, but it helps "protect" the light-streak from being darkened by other colors to come. It also helps you keep a complete range of lights and darks.

   Besides using white for lighter areas, you must mix black with your colors in places which should be darker. You'll mix in other colors as well. Look closely at a green can and you might see yellow-green or blue-green reflected there. Blend your crayons into a rich, waxy mixture. If you don't like the results, scrape away the layers and try again.

Dented Can Drawing

Food For Thought

1. Have you suggested a cast shadow on the "ground," so your can doesn't appear to be cut out and pasted onto the white paper?

2. Have you rounded the cylinder with shading to give form to the shape?

3. Have you used a full range of values from lightest to darkest?

Teacher's Tip

- Here is some helpful advice:

    First, be sure the cans are dry inside.

    Second, remind the kids that some restraint is necessary when they are about to "dent" their cans (they often want to smash them to smithereens).

> **"There is no love sincerer than the love of food."**
> George Bernard Shaw

À La Carte Art: Snack Attack Still Life

- Intermediate Cuisine to Advanced Gourmet
- Best Finished Later
- Artful Use of Leftovers
- Easy Clean Up!

What do kids love more than candy, chips, and soda pop? Other fast-food favorites include french fries, burgers, pizza, cookies, rolls, ice cream, and fruit. It's captivating cuisine!

Create a still life using the items from your next snack or lunch—you'll be consumed by your subject and vice-versa! Serve up some excitement with this project …it's icing on the cake.

> **"H**unger is the teacher of the arts and the inspirer of invention."
>
> Persius

Directions for Snack-Attack Still Life

1. **ARRANGE** about 5 objects in a group. Use an empty pop can, clean milk or juice container, drinking straw, napkin, wrapper, bag, etc. You can partly peel fruit or take a bite out of it. You can tear bags and crumple wrappers. Artfully add a piece of a candy bar or sprinkle a few snack chips about.

2. When your arrangement is an interesting but well-balanced grouping, begin to **SKETCH** it on white drawing paper that is 12" x 18" or larger. Press lightly with your pencil. Draw a "horizon line" too (the back edge of the desk-top) so that your objects do not appear to float.

3. Pay close attention to **DETAIL**. Take your time and notice the folds and wrinkles in paper and other small particulars. Only when the realistic drawing is complete are you ready to add color and values.
   NOTE: This work of art should take more than one session to finish. Secure your arrangement of objects in a safe place, wrap and refrigerate any perishables if necessary.

4. For **COLOR**, choose from crayons, colored pencils, markers, or oil pastels. Press heavily as you work, mixing and blending in a rich overlay of colors. Aim for a full range of values from the whitest highlights to the darkest shades. Remember to cast shadows on the table-top.

Snack-Attack Still Life

Food for Thought

1. In arranging your <u>composition</u> (organized grouping), did you use some overlapping to add unity?

2. In coloring, did you use many <u>tints</u> (light colors), middle values, and shades?

3. Do your forms appear three-dimensional?

4. Did you include a lot of realistic detail?

Teacher's Tip

- Here's your opportunity to discuss nutrition and empty calories! Combine this project with a unit on well-balanced meals. Today's pyramid of five food groups is topped with fats, oils, and sweets—and there's no "requirement" for candy bars! Put your composers and writers to work on songs about good foods, and then give a performance for other classes. Make up some jingles that reveal the shortcomings of junk food. Create posters promoting good foods and discouraging junk foods.

- If you must indulge in sweets, here's a scientific way to use them: Create the Earth! You'll need a clear plastic cup, a spoon, a large gumball, a piece of fudge, a vanilla wafer, 3 colors of sprinkles, some custard, and some frosting. First, study a diagram of the inside of the Earth. Using the hard gumball as the core, mold the fudge around it to act as the liquid metal layer. Spoon a little custard into the cup and then lay your inner/outer core on top. Spoon the rest of the pudding over that. The custard represents hot solid and molten rock. The vanilla wafer, representing the earth's crust, could hold a "mountain" on its surface. Build this "mountain" on the cookie with frosting. The Earth's 3 kinds of rocks—igneous, metamorphic, and sedimentary—are represented by the 3 colors of sprinkles. Place them on your frosting, balance the cookie on top of the custard, and you've made the Earth!

Divide and Conquer:
A Cross-Section Drawing

- Advanced Gourmet
- Best Finished Later

This still life drawing is different—a cut above the rest! You'll need drawing pencils, an eraser, and 12" x 18" white drawing paper. You'll also need fruit or vegetable subject matter: peppers, tomatoes, pumpkin, squash, pomegranates, cantaloupe, or anything else with an interesting-looking seed cavity. This project requires that the object be halved with a sharp knife, so it is not for young children.

A pleasing variation of this activity can be done on gray paper with black charcoal. Add white chalk highlights (they look great!) but take care to keep them "clean." If allowed to smear into the charcoal, the highlights become a muddy gray. When the works of art are done, spray them with fixative.

Any way you slice it, this is an idea you can really "sink your teeth into."

Cross Section Drawing Directions

1. **FIRST**, draw your fruit or vegetable while it's still whole. Place the drawing somewhat off-center on your page. If the object is quite small, draw it larger than life. Note the texture of the skin. Is it smooth and shiny, bumpy, webbed with a pattern like netting? Copy the surface quality as closely as you can.

2. **NEXT**, cut the object into halves and add a cross-section to your drawing. Place it at a slight angle to the other drawing, even overlapping it a bit if you wish. Closely observe the details, like the pulp and the seeds. Are there any hollow spaces? Is there stringy material? Take your time and add the particulars to your drawing.

3. **FINALLY**, use light and shadow to add realism. The white paper must show through wherever you want highlights to remain. For darker areas, press harder with your pencil (especially in the deepest-shaded parts). Remember to cast shadows on the "ground." Soften and blend your pencil shading with either your fingers or a tortillon (a blending stump).

Cross Section Drawing

Food for Thought

1. Is the overall tone of the drawing too pale, without any deeply-shaded accents?

2. Are the objects "floating" in a sea of white paper, or are they "grounded" with a horizon line and/or cast shadows?

3. Is attention to detail given?

Teacher's Tip

• For the distribution of halved fruits and vegetables to students, you might use paper plates or heavy folded newspapers to hold the produce. For continuing the work on another day, store the items in a refrigerator to keep them fresh.

PART II
Art You Can't Eat

Generally, neither the materials nor the finished works of art in this section are meant for human consumption.

Sometimes you just can't eat the art . . .

Make Color Magic

- It's Alimentary
- Minutes in the Making

Explore the wonderful world of color—use the primary colors to make a multitude of other colors. To try this experiment, you'll need some items from the kitchen: food coloring, clear glass or plastic containers of water, spoon, and measuring cup.

Add a drop or two of food coloring (either red, yellow, or blue) to a container of water.

After you have created three containers of primary-colored waters, make secondary colors either by pouring equal amounts of two colored waters together or by adding another food coloring. Remember: when you mix two primaries, you get another color.

Blue + Yellow = Green

Red + Yellow = Orange

Red + Blue = Purple

The mixed colors: green, orange, and purple, are the <u>secondaries</u>.

What happens if you mix twice as much blue as yellow to make green? This is a great way to learn about measurements and about the six <u>intermediate</u> colors, too!

Teacher's Tip

- Here's a fun and easy color project for teachers of early childhood. Put mustard into a clear zip-locking plastic bag and seal. Youngsters can press with their fingers on the outside, moving the mustard around to make designs. Erase the "fingerpainting" by smoothing out the bag. Add a bit of catsup to the contents and see how red and yellow make lovely variations of orange!

Food Coloring Can Fool You!

- It's Alimentary
- Minutes in the Making

Fold a piece of waxed paper in half, and then open the creased paper again. Squirt a drop of red food coloring onto the paper. Do the same with a drop of blue and a drop of yellow. Close the paper again and press with your fingers, mixing the colors a bit. If you work on top of a light-colored surface, you'll see a lovely creation forming inside the waxed paper "sandwich."

Open the paper once more and—fooled you!—the colors seem to almost disappear! The liquid food coloring has beaded up into very small droplets.

To make a "stained glass" artwork, an older child or an adult could press the folded waxed paper with a warm iron to seal the two layers. Put the finished piece in the window or mount it on white paper.

Tye-Dyed Tissue

- It's Alimentary
- Minutes in the Making

For this project, you'll need shallow containers of food coloring mixed with a little water. You'll also need newspapers and either white tissue paper, coffee filters, or plain white paper napkins.

Fold the white tissue several times, and then dip the edges or points into the colorants. Use several different colors in different "corners" of your tissue. Allow it to dry on the newspaper before unfolding.

Simple but stunning—a colorful creation!

Savor the Senses

- Alimentary to Advanced Gourmet
- Done in an Hour

When one is blindfolded, only four of the five senses remain usable: hearing, touch, smell, and taste. You can help others explore those attributes by arranging several "tests" for them.

Tantalizing Taste Test

To investigate the sense of taste, find five opaque (not transparent) containers with lids. Put sour cherry balls, lemon drops, "jawbreakers," malted milk balls, multi-flavored gum balls, or other round edibles similar in size in separate containers.

Ask your subjects to wash their hands before beginning the test. Then ask them to leave the room, with only one person remaining while the tests are being conducted. Next, blindfold your first "guinea pig" and begin. The subject may rattle the containers, feel what's inside, and taste a sample of each.

Is the sample soft or hard, crunchy or chewy? Is it sweet? Sour? Salty? Bland, sharp, rich, or bitter? It is not permitted to spit the tasted sample back into the container!

Many taste-testers will identify some of the mystery flavors correctly. With this game, as with the next two, your subjects may be allowed to watch subsequent test-takers if they promise to not give away any answers!

Guess the Scent

To challenge the sense of smell, assemble a variety of aromatic items from the kitchen: vanilla, ground coffee, sour milk, lemon, chili powder, cinnamon, cooked cabbage, cloves, chocolate, maple flavoring, orange, etc.

Blindfolded, your participant attempts to guess the scents correctly. Ask: "Does the sample remind you of anything? Is it pleasant, neutral, disgusting? How does it make you feel?"

Terrifying Touch Test—It's in the Bag

Approach this one with caution! There may be some cleaning up to do. Your "victim" will be subjected to samples concealed in opaque, leak-proof plastic bags. Use cold, cooked pasta in one, peeled grapes in another, and raw liver in yet another. More sample ideas include play-dough, cracked eggs, and sprouts. You can probably think of many more textures to handle.

Questions to ask: "Can you hold onto that sample or is it slippery? Is it hard, soft, wet, dry, smooth, rough? Does it feel pleasant or repulsive? What does it make you think of?"

Be sure your players wash their hands afterwards!

With any of the experiments above, you might ask your participants to write a descriptive paragraph detailing their feelings and reactions. Share the passages with the group.

Teacher's Tip

- When sighted students are blindfolded during the experiences above, they may come to a better understanding of the challenges faced by the visually impaired. Take this opportunity to discuss the matter.

> " *A*rt is the stored honey of the human soul . . . ."
>
> Theodore Dreiser

One-Color Collage

- It's Alimentary
- Done in an Hour
- Artful Use of Leftovers

If you were to celebrate the Vietnamese New Year (Tet), you might be served red fish or fish in red sauce. Red food is considered lucky—and any Vietnamese person who eats the fish's head and eyeballs will have the most luck!

Flip through any magazines that feature foods, and you'll find it easy to spot lots of red, orange, green, white, yellow, and brown. Foods in those colors are plentiful, while blue and purple foods are scarce (but not impossible to find)! Using a single color, create a collage based on cuisine. It's a delectable idea!

For a background, use 12" x 18" construction paper in the color you've chosen. Look through old magazines and find pictures of foods in your color. Cut them out or tear around their edges . It's fun to arrange the many pieces to fit together somewhat like a puzzle. You should use some overlapping, and you may have some printed words that show, too.

When you've filled the page with an artful arrangement, glue down all the pieces. Your one-color collage is complete!

One-Color Collage

Food For Thought

1. Did you use pictures with mostly the one color of choice?
2. Did you use a variety of sizes of foods?
3. Did you use good craftsmanship in cutting and gluing?

Teacher's Tip

- Three famous artists who created collages using papers are Pablo Picasso, Georges Braque, and Henri Matisse. Older students might research and write about the technique.

- Another foods collage idea: On a paper plate, a child can arrange and glue down a meal! Cut food photos from magazines, determine a balanced meal, and glue the items onto the plate. Do one for breakfast, one for lunch, and one for dinner. Do the foods appear pleasant together? Would the tastes go well together? A different version is to use colored construction paper to create one's own foods rather than cutting out magazine pictures. For example, purple circles represent grapes, brown strips stand for bacon, and a golden circle is a muffin.

- Here's a suggestion for early childhood teachers: Make a pizza puzzle. Use a pizza box and a cardboard pizza circle. Cut out food photos and glue them to the circle, covering the entire piece of round cardboard. Either laminate the circle or coat it with Mod-Podge (clear acrylic). Let it dry, and then cut it into puzzle pieces. Store your tasty puzzle in the pizza box.

Printmaking with Produce

- Alimentary to Intermediate Cuisine
- Minutes in the Making

Fruits and veggies can be used to stamp colorful designs onto paper. You'll need a knife, a variety of produce, liquid tempera paints in shallow containers, and white or colored construction paper. Newspapers covering your work area will aid in clean up. Another good idea is to wear a paint shirt or smock.

Here's a "shopping list" of just some of the fruits and vegetables you might try:

Celery	Avocado	Carrot
Onion	Pepper	Grapefruit
Apple	Mushroom	Orange
Pear	Lemon	Cauliflower

Arrange containers of paint (pie tins are excellent containers) in your work space, and use a knife to halve your assortment of printing "tools." Younger artists need adult help with this. If you choose to print on white or pastel paper, then press your produce into darker colors of paint. If your paper is a deep, dark color, choose white and light-colored tempera to print.

You might stamp a shape more than once without re-dipping it in paint—sometimes the second or "ghost" print is more appealing than the first! Choose paint colors that are pleasant together, and repeat them in a balanced fashion. Don't smear, but lift your fruit or vegetable instead. You may overlap shapes if desired. Try several different prints.

When your prints are done you'll need space to allow them to dry. When they are dry, these colorful pieces of art can stand on their own merit or they can be embellished. Use oil pastels to heavily outline and fill in some of the negative space (background). Keep your color scheme in mind as you do so. The enhanced prints will be palatable indeed!

Potato Prints Charming

- Advanced Gourmet
- Done in an Hour

Review safety rules before carving potato halves with paring knives or craft knives.

Use a baking potato, as it has less moisture than a general-purpose potato. Cut in half and let the cut sides stand on a paper towel to blot for a bit. Then cut away part of the potato surface, leaving a raised design. This simple, flat shape, in <u>relief</u> (projecting higher than the background), will print "backwards," or reversed. It can be stamped again and again to make a pattern.

To coat the carving with pigment before printing, choose from several methods. Use a brayer (printing roller) to roll on water-based printing ink, or simply paint the potato's printing surface with acrylics applied by brush. Another option is to make a stamp pad of several thicknesses of paper towels folded into a shallow container. Soak them with slightly thinned tempera paint and you have a paint pad!

Potato prints can be particularly striking if done on sheets of discontinued wallpaper. Select non-vinyl samples with simple patterns for the best results.

Great Gadget Prints

- Alimentary to Intermediate Cuisine
- Done in an Hour

Be a smart cookie at Christmas time and try printmaking with holiday cookie cutters. Wear a smock or paint shirt to protect your clothing. Stamp colored papers, large sheets of tissue-paper, or even newsprint! Use seasonal colors of tempera, and the results can become Christmas wrap (or make greeting cards on smaller papers). What great holiday fare!

Printing with kitchen utensils is not limited to the holiday. Use tools such as potato mashers and dessert molds to make nifty prints any time.

Printmaking

Food For Thought

1. Is the placement of each impression pleasing, with or without overlapping?

2. Have you used repetition of shapes and colors to add unity to the print?

3. Are the contrasts (differences of light and dark) good?

Teacher's Tip

- Some prehistoric cave art of 25,000 years ago used printmaking! The artist of ancient times sometimes smeared his hand with pigment and pressed it against a cave wall.

- Potato prints have been around a long time, but potatoes themselves were discovered by Spanish explorers in the Andes of South America in the sixteenth century. They brought them back to Europe, where potatoes were slowly accepted. Now they're a staple—a basic food in the diets of many people. Potato plants are tubers, which means they grow underground.

- If you cut fresh beets, parsnips, or carrots for printing tools, save the tops with one or two inches of the vegetable below. Put the tops in a shallow plate with some water, and place it all in a sunny spot. Keep watering and green shoots will grow!

- While fish are a far cry from vegetables, they make a great print! Rinse the fish, pat it dry, and lay it out on newspapers. Use a brayer to roll water-based ink all over the face-up side of the fish. Gently place thin paper (typing paper will work) over the fish, and press all over it with the palm of your hand. Peel off the paper to see your fish print.

Bird Food Fun

- Alimentary to Intermediate Cuisine
- Minutes in the Making
- Easy Clean Up!

We've been working with plenty of people foods. This project is for the birds!

Birdseed pretzels are easy to make and a great way to attract a flock of feathered friends. All you need are the following:

- waxed paper
- nontoxic white glue in a squeeze bottle
- birdseed or sunflower seeds

Squirt the glue onto a flat sheet of the waxed paper, "drawing" fat glue lines into pretzel-like shapes. Be sure to make the glue lines wide enough (over $1/4$ inch). Also be sure to make all the glue lines in a single pretzel touch each other, just as real pretzels do.

Generously sprinkle the seeds onto the glue . Later, you can lift the waxed paper and pour off the extra seeds to be used again.

Allow your pretzels to dry for a day or two. Then carefully peel away the pretzels from the waxed paper. Hang the birds' bounty outdoors on tree branches and watch the birds binge!

Sandpainting With Salt

- Intermediate Cuisine to Advanced Gourmet
- Done in an Hour

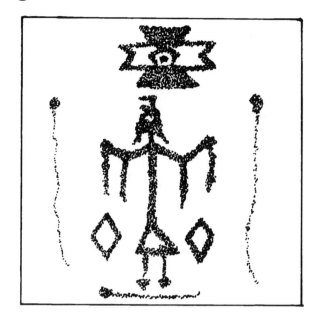

Authentic Pueblo and Navaho sandpainting, or drypainting, is done for religious reasons and is temporary. Colored sands are trickled upon a smooth sandbed on the floor of the hogan, or upon a soft buckskin. Symbolic line, form, and color are used.

The production of our own "sand" design is not meant to copy sacred rituals. Those ceremonial paintings are created specifically for certain occasions and are then destroyed. Those works, made with such strong feeling, can inspire us to make our own versions with our own favorite symbols.

Ready to make a sensational sand painting? You'll need table salt or canning salt, containers with lids, food coloring, glue in a squeeze bottle, and cardboard or matboard.

First, prepare the colored sand. To several tablespoons of salt in a lidded container, add five or six drops of food coloring. Shake vigorously and <u>voila</u>! Indian artists customarily use red, yellow, white, and black pigments, as well as mixtures.

Sandpainting Directions

First, you may choose to sketch your design lightly in pencil on the cardboard background. Traditional <u>motifs</u> (themes) include tall figures, plants, rainbows, serpents, arrows, and lightning.

Next, squeeze out lines and shapes of glue for all the parts of your design that you wish to be one particular color. Sprinkle that color of salt into the glue—make sure all the glue is well-covered by salt. Then, tip your cardboard slightly, tap gently, and pour off the excess. If you catch the surplus salt on a tray or a large sheet of paper, you can reuse it.

Repeat the process for each color of "sand" in your design.

After the rite, when genuine sandpaintings have served their purpose, they are destroyed. You may want to save yours as a reminder of a rich Native American heritage.

Teacher's Tip

- <u>Iikay</u> ("where the gods come and go") is the Navaho word for sand painting.

- Colored rice can be substituted for salt. Add food coloring to $\frac{1}{4}$ cup water, mix in $\frac{1}{2}$ cup rice and let sit for about 5 minutes. Then pour out the water using a sieve. Spread the colored rice out on newspapers to dry.

  Rather than cardboard as a support for this project, try sandpaper for "authenticity."

  Ideally, as students complete each color of "sand," they would give it time to set before going on to the next color.

Sand Layers in a Jar

- Intermediate Cuisine to Advanced Gourmet
- Done in an Hour

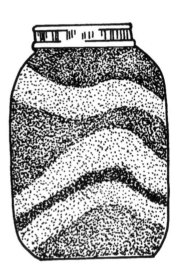

Fill a jar with a rainbow! You'll need a variety of colors of salt or rice, a nicely-shaped clear jar with a lid, and a spoon and/or a Popsicle stick.

First, pour a layer of colored "sand" into the jar. It may be level in the bottom of your jar, or it may be uneven. Next, add a layer of a different colored "sand." This layer may be sloping in another direction. Continue adding layers, and vary the depths of the layers. You may add even more interest by pushing a stick along the edge of the glass through several layers, using a down-and-up motion.

Another technique to try is using your spoon or stick to create "waves" or even zig-zags in a layer, all the way around the glass wall. Wow!

Continue adding layers until you reach the very top of the jar. Screw the lid on carefully and do not shake the jar!

Teacher's Tip

- Sand layers could be a scientific model of sedimentary rock. Discuss causes of sediment, look at photos of the layered sandstone and limestone of the Grand Canyon, and make your own model of Earth's ancient layers.

- Here's another science activity—one that's done with salt and pepper.

  Scatter some salt and ground pepper together on a table top. Rub a plastic spoon with a wool cloth and hold the spoon an inch or so over the mixture. Because the pepper is lighter in weight than the grains of salt, it rises more easily to the negatively-charged spoon.

Funny Foods

(Illustrating Idioms)

- Intermediate Cuisine
- Minutes in the Making
- Easy Clean Up!

Does a french fry wear a beret? Does angel food cake have wings and a halo? <u>Idioms</u> are phrases or expressions peculiar to a language, and their meanings may be very different from the literal. For example, if you tell someone he is "driving you up the wall," you both know he's not actually chasing you up the wallpaper!

We can use idioms that apply to certain foods to create witty illustrations. For instance, strawberries are not really made of straw, but we could portray them as such. Other foods that could be humorously pictured literally are string beans, hot dogs, and pancakes! You can think of many more "funny foods." Use pencils, crayons, or markers on white drawing paper to illustrate some "funny foods" of your own.

"*Hunger is the teacher of the arts and the inspirer of invention.*"

Persius

Creative Kitchen Clays

Do-It-Yourself Dough

- Alimentary to Intermediate Cuisine
- Best Finished Later

This play-dough recipe requires no cooking. Add together:

- 2 cups flour
- 1 cup salt
- $\frac{1}{2}$ cup water

Mix all ingredients together in a large bowl, and then knead the mixture with your hands. If you wish to add color, blend in food coloring. Other colorants to try are powdered flavored gelatins, colored powdered drink mixes, or powdered tempera (not to be eaten).

You may store this clay in a labeled and covered container in the refrigerator if you wish.

Just as potter's clay can be fired in a kiln, this clay can be "fired" in a kitchen oven! While the making of the clay can be done by children, the baking should be done by an adult.

Teacher's Tip

- The Do-It-Yourself Dough recipe makes a nice white or colored dough, but you can make it interesting with the addition of 2 cups of used coffee grounds. Substitute leftover coffee for the water in the recipe, too. This adds a nice color and speckles to the dough. Artwork made with this stuff almost looks as if it were made of stone!

Wonder Dough

- Intermediate Cuisine to Advanced Gourmet
- Best Finished Later

This white bread dough, like the previous recipe, requires no cooking. It is not recommended for very young children who might eat the sticky stuff!

Remove the crusts from several slices of white bread. Don't throw the crusts away— feed them to the birds! Rip the bread into tiny pieces, place them in a bowl, and add a tablespoon of white glue. Mix with a fork until all the pieces are moistened, adding a bit more glue if necessary. Knead the mixture with your fingers until it becomes pliable.

White bread dough works best for small, delicate sculptures, earrings, buttons, or beads. Allow your objects to air-dry for a day or two. They will have a smooth, satin-like finish which you may enhance with a clear glaze if desired. Even clear nail polish will work!

The dough can be tinted with food coloring before it is used to shape objects, or it can be painted when it is dry. Extra dough should be refrigerated in a covered container. Add a few drops of peppermint oil to clay mixture that you plan to keep for awhile. It will keep the clay fresher and sweeter-smelling.

Ashanti Dolls

- Intermediate Cuisine to Advanced Gourmet
- Best Finished Later

The Ashanti people of Africa's Gold Coast, now called Ghana, were renowned craftsmen. One type of ornament meant for Ashanti women or girls was an "akua-ba" doll, which is a small figure carried in the pocket or worn around the neck.

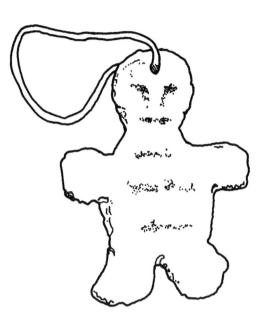

You can make an akua-ba doll from the Do-It-Yourself Dough recipe, and then harden it in the oven.

When the clay has been made, flatten it out to about $1/2$" thick. Use a tool such as a pencil or a popsicle stick to form the head, body, and details. Don't make the neck too thin! Keep the facial features simplified.

Make a hole near the top if the doll will be worn as a necklace. Dry the figure on waxed paper for several days, or harden it on a cookie sheet in the oven for several hours at 200 degrees.

Older children may lightly sand the dolls and paint them with acrylics or tempera. A final coat of clear acrylic spray will add a nice shine.

Teacher's Tip

- The Ashanti believed akua-ba dolls would aid in the birth of healthy, handsome children. The dolls had three basic head shapes: oval (believed to help bring a baby girl), square (a boy), and round (a wise baby).

Ancient crafts continue to flourish in and from Africa. Artistic expressions of tribal life are one way for Africans to pass on their cultural heritage to others.

Cooked Cornstarch Clay

- Alimentary to Intermediate Cuisine
- Best Finished Later

For this recipe, youngsters need the supervision of adults or older teens.

Stir together in a saucepan: 2 cups baking soda, 1 cup cornstarch, and $1\frac{1}{2}$ cups cold water. Stir until smooth.

Cook the mixture over medium heat until it thickens, stirring constantly. The mixture will lose its shine and become difficult to stir. Next, turn it out onto a plate and cover it with a damp cloth. When the clay has cooled, knead and form it into the desired shapes, or store it in a covered container in the refrigerator until ready to use. It keeps for about a week. The clay can be colored with food coloring.

After you have formed a small sculpture from the clay, let it dry at room temperature for several days. Then your artwork can be painted and protected with gloss medium if desired.

More Cooked Clay

- Alimentary to Intermediate Cuisine
- Best Finished Later

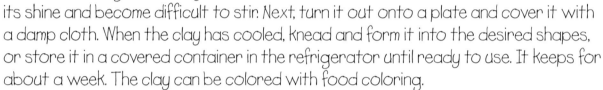

Cook up some fun with this recipe! Add together in a large saucepan: 3 cups of flour, $1\frac{1}{2}$ cups salt, 3 cups water, 2 tablespoons cooking oil, and 1 tablespoon cream of tartar. The mixture must be cooked slowly and stirred constantly. When the clay comes away from the side of the pan and becomes very stiff, remove it from the pan. Let cool, and then knead until smooth.

Form sculptures with your hands, or use a rolling pin, cookie cutters, and other utensils to shape and cut the clay. To produce interesting patterns, stamp and press the clay with a spatula, or garlic press. Your creations will harden on standing.

Keep the clay in tightly-sealed containers to prevent its drying out. You can rejuvenate dried-out dough by adding a few drops of cooking oil or water.

Play-Dough Pizza

#5

- Intermediate Cuisine to Advanced Gourmet
- Done in an Hour

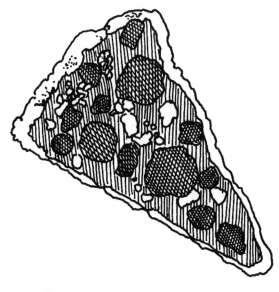

Sausage, peppers, cheese—yum! Use play-clay to concoct a delicious-looking pizza—thin crust or deep-dish. Use a rolling pin for thin crust; hand-"toss" the deep dish.

Knead red, yellow, and green food coloring into separate batches of dough. Make brown by mixing red and green together.

Now form "pepperoni" discs, "green pepper" bits, "onion," "tomato sauce," and more. You might wish to add sprinkles of egg noodles for "cheese."

Pizza, anyone?

Cinnamon Dough

#6

- Alimentary to Intermediate Cuisine
- Done in an Hour

Make a sweet-smelling dough on the stove (adult supervision, again!). You'll need:

- 1 cup ground cinnamon
- $1\frac{1}{2}$ to 2 cups flour
- 2 cups water
- saucepan, spoon, and rolling pin

Bring the water to a boil, remove from heat, and stir in the cinnamon. Add the flour slowly, stirring well. When the dough has sufficiently cooled, knead it. Flour the work surface and roll out the dough with a rolling pin. Use your hands to form figurines or small sculptures, or use cookie cutters to make ornaments. If you wish to hang the ornaments, be sure to make a hole near the top. After drying for several days, your pieces may be hung with fish line—they'll scent the breeze!

"The recipe that is not shared will soon be forgotten, but ones that are shared will be enjoyed by future generations."
– Unknown

Remarkable Recipes for Paint and Paste

The next few pages are devoted to ways of making a medley of homemade mixtures. Go ahead and create a concoction or blend up a brew. First, let's prepare a potpourri of paints ...

Wacky Watercolors

- Advanced Gourmet
- Best Finished Later

Hundreds of years ago, the first paints were made of natural color particles held together with animal fat or eggs. Today, store-bought watercolors are wonderful, and you can make your own colorful cakes of paint. You'll need:

- 2 tablespoons each of white vinegar, cornstarch, and baking soda
- 1 teaspoon corn syrup
- food coloring
- small containers
- small bottle lids

Mix the vinegar and baking soda to make a fascinating fizz. When the hissing stops, add the cornstarch and corn syrup. Blend the mixture. Then divide it into containers, and add a few drops of food coloring to each. You may use these paints immediately or pour them into tiny lids to dry into cakes.

Powdered-Milk Paint

- Intermediate Cuisine
- Minutes in the Making

This paint has a shiny finish when dry. It cleans up with water.

Mix $1/2$ cup powdered nonfat milk with $1/2$ cup water in a container. Add enough powdered tempera to achieve the opacity (lack of transparency) desired. Store tightly covered in the refrigerator.

Egg Tempera

- Intermediate Cuisine
- Minutes in the Making

This paint can be thinned and cleaned up with water, but is quite permanent when dry. Store covered in the refrigerator and use within several days.

You will need twice as much egg yolk as water, so break several egg yolks into a measuring cup first. Then add half as much water and mix well. Use a portion of this base mixed with powdered or liquid tempera in a separate container for each color desired.

Next, a group of glue recipes:

First-Rate Flour Paste

- Intermediate Cuisine
- Minutes in the Making

You'll need one cup flour, one cup water, a bowl, and a spoon. Begin with a small amount of flour and water, mix them together until smooth, and then add more of either ingredient as needed. This makes a good papier-mâché paste. Refrigerate any leftover paste you wish to use later.

Rice Paste (or Finger Paint)

- Intermediate Cuisine
- Best Finished Later

This thick paste is perfect for tissue collages because it dries clear. To convert it into finger paint, just add food coloring or powdered tempera.

Put $1/4$ cup dry instant rice into a bowl and add $1/2$ cup water. Let it set overnight.

The next day, use an electric mixer and blend the rice with $1/2$ cup hot water. Let the mixture cool, and store in a covered glass jar. A teaspoon of antiseptic (such as Listerine) may retard spoilage if added to the mixture.

Homemade Casein Glue

- Intermediate to Advanced Gourmet
- Best Finished Later

Casein (pronounced "kay-see-in") is an acid substance produced in the curdling of milk. It is used in, among other things, waterproof glues and certain paints. To make this glue you'll need:

- 2 cups skim milk
- 4 teaspoons vinegar
- 4 teaspoons baking soda
- 2 tablespoons warm water
- a sieve
- a fork
- a pan
- a covered jar

Heat the milk and vinegar in the pan, stirring constantly. The milk should become lumpy with curds. Strain out the liquid (the whey), add the warm water, and stir in the baking soda. Smash the lumps with the fork and force the mixture through the sieve into the jar. Let sit, covered, for 24 hours. Stir before using.

Special Glue for Stickers or Stamps

- Alimentary to Intermediate Cuisine
- Done in an Hour

Make your own "postage stamps" or stickers from glossy magazine pictures. Dissolve one part gelatin (either flavored gelatin mix or unflavored gelatin) in two parts hot water. Stir until dissolved, and spread on the backs of small pictures you've cut from magazines. When dry, flatten them with a heavy book if they've curled up. To use, just lick as you would a real stamp and apply to paper!

Fantasy Food Faces

- Intermediate Cuisine
- Done in an Hour
- Easy Clean Up!

His works are weird and wonderful! Guiseppe Arcimboldo was a sixteenth-century Italian painter from Milan who used fruits and vegetables, flora, and fauna to compose human heads in his work. His paintings are bizarre and clever transformations.

Arcimboldo is best known, perhaps, for two series that he painted: One was made up of the four seasons (with the appropriate crops) and the other represented the elements of earth, air, fire and water. You, too, can create portraits that are <u>composites</u> (combinations, made up of various parts). You'll be amazed at the fruits of your imagination—and the vegetables, too!

If you need more inspiration, look through seed catalogs for ideas.

This idea really bears fruit, but a variation is to use the animal kingdom for a fanciful face, as Arcimboldo sometimes did. His "Air" is formed by a mass of birds; his "Water" is filled with undersea creatures (crustaceans, mollusks, and amphibians).

Whether it's animals or a fruit-and-vegetable face, this is an idea ripe for the picking. Plant the seeds of your creativity!

Fantasy Food Faces Directions

1. As you prepare to draw a portrait in the style of Arcimboldo's, remember that not only should you represent the features of the face but also the forms. Features are eyes, nose, mouth, ears, and brows. The forms of the cheekbones, chin, and forehead must also be included.

   Imagine eyes made of grapes, a nose made from a carrot, and eyebrows of green beans! A cheek might remind you of an apple, and a jawbone and chin might resemble a squash. You can even draw fruits in sections or halved if you wish—a slice of watermelon could become a mouth!

2. Use 12" x 18" white paper the "tall" way—up-and-down. Decide whether your face will be a profile (side view) or front view. Lightly sketch your fantasy face in pencil first. You can make a man, woman, or child, and you can even add a hat, a tie, eyeglasses, or jewelry. Don't forget hair! A beard or a moustache is okay, too.

3. When your drawing is done, outline it with a thin black marker and use colored markers, colored pencils, or crayons to finish your work.

Here's a list of just some of the fruits and vegetables you might choose for your fantasy face:

artichokes	brussels sprouts	celery	olives
bananas	cabbage	corn	onions
beans	cantaloupe	cucumber	parsley
beets	carrots	eggplant	peaches
blueberries	cauliflower	lettuce	pears
broccoli	cherries	zucchini	peas
peppers	raspberries	pineapple	rhubarb
pumpkin	spinach	radishes	strawberries

Figure Collage After Arcimboldo

- Intermediate Cuisine
- Done in an Hour
- Artful Use of Leftovers

A modification of the previous portraits is to create an entire figure with foods—photos of foods, that is. You'll need old magazines, scissors, glue, and paper.

Use 12" x 18" paper for a background. Use it vertically (the tall way). Decide whether you wish to make a front or a side view of your character. Begin by cutting out pictures of edibles and arranging them to form trunk, head, limbs, hands, and feet. Clothing, hair, and accessories are fun. Hats, ties, jewelry, and eyeglasses are just some of the possibilities for accessories.

Finally, glue down all the pieces and you have a great guy or gal made from goodies!

Want to give the words "fish food" a whole new meaning? This activity could be adapted to call for other fanciful creatures besides humans: fish, insects, and birds might be assembled from food photos. Cultivate creativity with a collage!

Fantasy Food Collages

Food For Thought

1. Have you worked large enough on the paper, creating an impressive collage?
2. Is there enough detail for a lot of interest?
3. Is good craftsmanship evident in the cutting and gluing?
4. Is the piece inventive and humorous?

ANSWERS, Ripped Shopping List Game (page 63)

1. apple
2. bacon
3. blueberries
4. butter
5. carrots
6. fish
7. grapes (or grapefruit)
8. lettuce
9. margarine
10. noodles
11. oranges
12. peaches
13. potatoes
14. radishes
15. strawberries
16. tomatoes
17. yogurt
18. zucchini

Student's Name: _____

Ripped Shopping List Game

Grocery lists make the task of shopping much easier. Unfortunately, this shopping list was torn in several places, leaving only a few letters from each item to be purchased. Fortunately, the items are in alphabetical order, which will help you identify each one.

1. _____ pples

2. _____ aco _____

3. _____ ueber _____

4. _____ utter

5. _____ arro _____

6. _____ ish

7. _____ rap _____

8. _____ tuce

9. _____ rgari _____

10. _____ oodl _____

11. _____ range

12. _____ ches

13. _____ tatoe _____

14. _____ adishe _____

15. _____ trawbe _____

16. _____ omato _____

17. _____ ogurt

18. _____ cchin _____

Hoagies and Heroes

- It's Alimentary
- Done in an Hour
- Artful Use of Leftovers

Dagwoods, subs, grinders—whatever you call these giant sandwiches, they're the best. And the BIGGEST!

Relish some excitement? Use colored construction paper scraps to build a super sandwich. First cut out a big (paper) bun or two pieces of "bread." Glue the bottom piece of your sub to a 12" x 18" paper background, near the bottom of the sheet.

Now for the "stuffing!" Find colored papers with which to create ham, salami, turkey, bacon, meatballs, pepperoni, steak, bologna, roast beef, or seafood. Layer your fillings with paper cheeses, onions, lettuce, tomatoes, pickles, olives, sprouts, and peppers. Don't forget to cut out and add such condiments as yellow paper mustard, red for catsup, or white for mayo or cream cheese. Stack your sandwich so that all the goodies can be seen. Arrange the pieces before you glue them down.

Finally, top the towering masterpiece with the upper piece of paper bread or bun (wheat, rye, or white). It looks good enough to eat!

Teacher's Tip

- Consider green and yellow-green tissue paper for "lettuce"—when crinkled, it closely resembles the real thing!

"Sometimes I've believed as many as six impossible things before breakfast."

Lewis Carroll

Pasta Pictures, Noodle Jewels, & Bean Balls

Pastas are so common with Italian meals that they are often served as the first course. The exact beginnings of pasta are unknown, although ancient Romans made and ate it.

Pastas are available in many attractive forms. There are string or ribbon pastas, stars, elbows, shells, twists, rings, nuggets, pinwheels, tubes, and bows. There's orzo, which looks like rice. There are pasta alphabet letters, baseballs and bats, and jack-o-lanterns! Colorful pasta bears and dinosaurs are available, made from dehydrated vegetables. See what's "in store" for you! The pastabilities are endless.

Gather an assortment of pasta products and make a mosaic. Use a piece of cardboard or colored matboard as the background for a "delicious" design.

Pasta Pictures

- Alimentary to Intermediate Cuisine
- Done in an Hour

Mosaic is an art form that was very popular during the Byzantine period (about the sixth century to the eighth). Traditionally, a mosaic is a design made of small pieces of colored glass, ceramic, or stone, set in cement or adhesive. Each piece is set separately, with a small space between each one.

Ready to start your mosaic masterpiece? First, arrange the noodles, spaghetti, and macaroni into a pleasing composition before gluing them down. Use an interesting variety of sizes, shapes, and thicknesses of pasta. Small pieces might be better adhered by first spreading glue in an area of the background and then sprinkling the pieces into the glue.

You can even dye the pasta with food coloring or watercolors ahead of time, although the natural colors are very nice as they are.

The mosaic you make is probably non-objective—it doesn't represent anything recognizable from life. But you can create a pasta picture that is representational, if you wish. Arrange (on your sturdy background) a recognizable scene. Use pasta shells for a beach scene or an underwater one. Try using "wheels" for vehicles, pasta tubes for logs, or bows for butterflies.

Exercise your imagination! Use your noodle and work up an appetite for fun! If desired, coat the finished project (when the glue is dry) with polymer medium or plastic spray.

Pasta Mosaic

Food For Thought

1. Do the colors of the background and the macaroni products work well together?

2. Is there a center of interest?

3. Does the background show through more in some areas and hardly at all in others, for variety?

Teacher's Tip

- Pasta has been a treasured delicacy in Italy for over 700 years. Want to learn some Italian? <u>Orecchiette</u> means "little ears," <u>ziti</u> is "bridegrooms," <u>linguine</u> means "small tongues," and <u>vermicelli</u>, "little worms."

- Check out the children's book "Oodles o' Noodles," by M. Roc and A. Stomann. It illustrates "lotsa" noodles!

- Classroom hints: Provide a pie plate, muffin tin, or egg carton for each child to hold a selection of pasta, seeds, beans or grains. Buy a bag of birdseed if you'd like a variety of seeds. Instead of colored matboard for a background, youngsters might use a paper plate or a styrofoam meat tray. The latter won't warp like cardboard might. Kids often want to build upward rather than working in relief. Decide in advance whether you will accept that.

- Pasta can even be cooked and used while soft, molded into a shape and allowed to harden again. As you sculpt, keep the rest of the pasta in water until you're ready to use it. Create line "drawings" from spaghetti—adhering it to a dark-colored matboard.

- Youngsters might like an interpretive dance in which they pretend to be spaghetti. Uncooked spaghetti is very stiff and straight. As it is placed in hot water it becomes softer, and when the water boils the strands might twirl and writhe. Finally, the water is strained out and the pasta is topped with sauce. What an imaginative exercise!

- Aural tip: Dried beans, seeds, and grains can be enclosed in small containers for great shakers or "maracas." Use rice, corn, and uncooked tapioca in clean, empty plastic jars, metal spice cans, small boxes, even soda pop cans with the openings taped shut. Experiment and see how many different sounds you can make. Shake them to music or to clapping. March or dance to the rhythm.

Noodle Jewels

- Alimentary to Intermediate Cuisine
- Best Finished Later

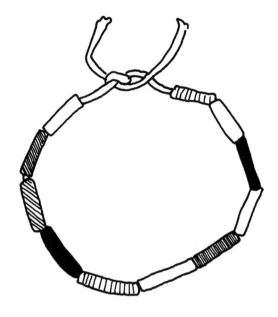

With the many types of dried pasta available today, you can thread a king's ransom in "jewels." Choose from shapes like wheels, bow-ties, tiny circles, and tubes. Make colorful bracelets and necklaces with pasta "beads."

First, shake the pasta in jars with a few drops of food coloring and a teaspoon of water. Remember that blue and red together make purple, orange is a mixture of red and yellow, and green is a combination of blue and yellow. Spread the colored beads on several layers of newspaper to dry.

For your string, use yarn, thin ribbon, nylon fishing line, or even shoelaces! Wrap the ends of yarn or ribbon with a piece of tape for ease in guiding it through the shapes. Or dip the yarn-ends in glue and let them dry for easier stringing. Work on a table and string each bead to the center of your line.

For added interest, you can thread old buttons or real beads between the pasta shapes. When you've strung the length you want, tie the ends in a triple knot. If you're really ambitious, you can make a garland for a Christmas tree!

Bean Balls

- Intermediate Cuisine
- Best Finished Later

Transform old tennis balls into outstanding ornaments! Cover them with red kidney beans, Great Northern beans, pinto beans, blackeye peas, and/or yellow or green split peas. Use your imagination! Painting the tennis balls first is optional (if you do, let dry before proceeding).

A low-temperature glue gun makes your work go faster, but if you use white glue instead, then do one area at a time and let dry. Nestle your beans closely for good coverage. Glue on a loop of ribbon for hanging, if desired.

These bean balls are beautiful, and that's "no hill of beans!"

Teacher's Tip

- Grow some sprouts from your leftover beans. You'll need a jar with a lid, a hammer and nail, and water. Punch holes in the lid with the nail, and then pour about an inch of dried beans into the jar. Add water to cover. Let the beans soak for about 6 hours. Put the lid on and let the water drain out of the holes. Place the jar in a dark cupboard and remember to wet the contents every day, pouring off the water each time. In about 4 days, you'll have sprouts!

More Mosaics

- Alimentary to Intermediate Cuisine
- Done in an Hour

Mosaics can be created from a great variety of materials, including many from the kitchen! Some materials to consider are seeds, grains, ground coffee, nut shells, popcorn, Indian corn, and dried peas or beans in different sizes and colors. There are yellow and green split peas, chick peas, lentils, red or white kidney beans, lima, pinto, navy, and black beans. Dry breakfast cereals come in many shapes and colors, too. Even eggshells can be crushed into pieces and glued into a mosaic. Use the eggshells in their natural colors, or dye them.

Kwanzaa Necklace

- Alimentary to Intermediate Cuisine
- Done in an Hour

Each December 26 marks the beginning of a seven-day African-American celebration called Kwanzaa (In Swahili, it means "first fruits of the harvest."). Its message is responsibility, unity, and self-love. It celebrates family, culture, and community. Other principles of Kwanzaa are self-determination, collective work, cooperative economics, and faith. Zawadi (gifts) are part of the festivities, too. In commemoration of the harvest, the community holds a karamu (feast). In honor of kuumba, or creativity, there might be dancing and the making of works of art. Songs are sung, gifts exchanged, and homemade necklaces worn. To make your own Kwanzaa necklace, paint some pasta in the customary colors of red, black, and green.

Thread them onto yarn or string and tie a knot.

Teacher's Tip

- If you commemorate Kwanzaa in the classroom, make it a multi-sensory experience with a scenic slide show, African music, and authentic scents and flavors!

- To add more variety to noodle necklaces, soak whole cloves and allspice for several days to soften them. Thread a needle with nylon thread and pierce the spices, alternating them with pasta. Another item to soak and string is the sunflower seed.

- Teachers of the very young might use colorful "O"-type cereal such as Froot Loops for stringing. A great candy necklace can be made by using "shoestring" licorice, strung with Lifesavers, and then knotted. Warning: this jewelry will survive only until the wearer gets hungry!

Beautiful Breakfast—A Feast for the Eyes

- Intermediate Cuisine to Advanced Gourmet
- Done in an Hour

Pancakes or waffles? Cereal or fruit? What do you eat for breakfast in the morning? No doubt about it, you need a nutritious start to a busy day. Many health professionals consider breakfast the most important meal.

Just some of the delicious morning fare that might be considered include toast, muffins, juice, eggs, ham, yogurt, peanut butter, and pizza. (Pizza?!) Other things that might be found on the breakfast table include milk and sugar, salt and pepper, butter, cutlery, napkins, place mats, dishware, mugs, tumblers, honey, and jelly.

Use some of these foods and objects in a drawing on 12" x 18" white paper. Work very lightly in pencil first, and draw each item as if it were made of transparent glass. Overlap each shape, too—such overlapping will add unity to the artwork (it will help tie the design together).

Draw about seven items in all, and add a "horizon" or a line representing the back edge of a tabletop.

After your sketched composition is complete, go over the pencil lines with a black crayon. Later we'll fill spaces in with watercolor paint, and the waxy black outlines will help keep the wet paint within each shape from spreading to others. Press hard with the black crayon!

Next, you'll need a container of water, a brush, and watercolor paints. You'll also need to know how to mix primary and secondary colors in order to create the six intermediate colors. Your assignment for this artwork is to use the intermediates only! Who says cocoa has to be brown and orange juice yellow? Aqua eggs and mauve oatmeal are really quite lovely!

On page 42 we made "magic" by mixing food coloring. Here's a list of the intermediate colors. Create each one by mixing together the two colors that make up the name:

red-orange	blue-violet	yellow-orange
blue-green	red-violet	yellow-green

Use the lid of your paint set for mixing. A common mistake is to not use enough water. Mix enough of an intermediate color to fill in several of the shapes in your work.

Finally, as you paint, remember that you should not cross over the black crayon lines. Rather than painting an entire item one color, try filling in only within a shape. This produces a pleasant "stained-glass" effect.

The intermediates are beautiful together. Your finished painting will glow with great color.

Beautiful Breakfast

Food For Thought

1. Have you used many different shapes and sizes in your drawing?

2. Did you paint neatly? For example, is your painting streaky or smooth? Did the colors run together?

3. Did you make true intermediate colors?

4. Did you use all 6 of the intermediates, each in several different places?

Teacher's Tip

- Don't be surprised at what some children consider appropriate for breakfast. Also, be prepared for lots of questions concerning the accuracy of students' intermediates: "Is my yellow-green too greenish? Does my red-orange need more red?" These questions are a good thing, actually!

  Remember that watercolor is a challenging medium which can be very frustrating. Using good-quality paints and brushes helps greatly, as does having paper towels handy. Many youngsters do not use enough water in their brushes, and they often mix up too little of a needed color to fill an entire shape.

  Some children will insist on painting toast brown and orange juice orange—they're literal souls who just can't tolerate the idea of blue-green milk! Also, some children will cross over their black outlines and paint an entire item one color. Expect these things, as surely as you know there'll be paint-drips!

- An accompanying project, perhaps for those who finish their paintings early, is to design a place mat on 13" x 18" heavy paper.

- For fun, why not color your breakfast for real? Use food coloring in the scrambled eggs or glass of milk! Read such books as "Green Eggs and Ham" by Dr. Seuss (Random House, 1960).

- Here's a great Web site with a variety of classroom ideas about nutrition: http://www.pork4kids.com. There's also information and recipes for children and parents.

Fun Batik with Flour

- Intermediate Cuisine to Advanced Gourmet
- Best Finished Later

Batik, or "wax painting," began in China or India over 2,000 years ago. It often involves a wax coating applied to parts of a fabric. When the cloth is dipped in various dyes, only the parts of the fabric unprotected by the wax take on the colors of the dyes.

The batik method we'll use, rather than wax resist, is a starch resist done with paste. In an African dye process named "adire eleko," a starch made from cassava flour is used. Africans call this starch "lafun." We'll use ordinary flour and watercolors for our batik.

You can use this terrific technique to create a wall-hanging, table runner, or mantle cloth. To begin, you'll need some cotton muslin from the fabric store. Buy either the bleached or the unbleached kind, and don't launder it before using. Tape the fabric, 9" x 12" or larger, to heavy cardboard. Attach masking tape to all four sides of the cloth, stretching it tight.

Next, mix up this recipe in a container:
- $\frac{1}{2}$ cup flour
- $\frac{1}{2}$ cup water
- 1 teaspoon alum

Apply your paste to the fabric with a stiff brush. You may either work directly (without guidelines) or you may have slipped heavily-blackened sketches between your cloth and the cardboard support. Such dark designs will show through the fabric to serve as a pattern as you apply the paste. Your design may be representational—authentic ones often use such implements as combs and mirrors or knives. Your patterns may be abstracted from real life or may be non-objective instead (not based on any object from life).

Besides applying the paste "freehand," another method is to cut stencils from tagboard to create a "masking" device. Use your stiff brush to paint the openings of the stencil with paste. Whether handpainted or stenciled, the starch designs must be set aside when finished, so they can dry overnight.

Wait one day before applying color to the cloth. Use large brushes to paint bright watercolors (or food coloring) onto the fabric. Use intense color because it will dry somewhat lighter. Colors used traditionally in Africa include red, yellow, brown, indigo blue, and black.

A distinguishing characteristic of batik is a "cobweb" effect caused by color flowing into cracks in the resist material. To accomplish that, paint over the entire cloth, designs and all. Press down on the paste-shapes as you paint. The hard paste will break up a bit and allow paint to seep into the fissures, adding an interesting "cracked" line.

After the painting is done and the cloth has dried thoroughly, chip off the paste to reveal the white shapes of your pattern. Use either your fingernails or a blunt knife to flake off the dried paste. Your batik beauty is not washable, but it can be pressed with a warm iron if you wish.

Teacher's Tip

- The Yoruba people of southwest Nigeria make adire eleko cloth using blue indigo dye.

  Some people, like the Yoruba, dip the fabric into a cool dye bath, rinse, and then scrape off the softened paste with a tool such as a table knife.

Puff-Paint

- Alimentary to Intermediate Cuisine
- Done in an Hour

This thick paint is perfect for the visually challenged who would like to feel the patterns they've created after the paint is dry.

Mix equal amounts of flour, salt, and water in a container. Add tempera paint until the desired color is achieved. Pour into clean plastic squeeze bottles, and squirt designs onto cardboard, matboard, or heavy paper. While it is still wet, you might sprinkle some glitter into the paint if desired.

> **"A** tale without love is like beef without mustard: insipid."
>
> Anatole France

Great Granny Apples

- Advanced Gourmet
- Best Finished Later

Make a "Granny" doll-head or a "Gramps" puppet with this time-honored technique.

You'll need the following:

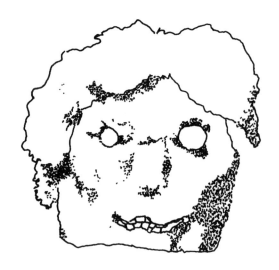

- a firm apple
- a paring knife
- cotton batting
- lemon juice
- round-headed pins
- salt
- spray varnish
- yarn, fabric scraps, glue

Peel and core the apple and stuff the center with cotton. Use the paring knife carefully to carve out eye and cheek hollows, and to form the nose, chin, and brows. Carve the features shallowly, without going too deep, as the hollows will deepen as the apple dries.

Next, dip the apple in lemon juice if you'd like to keep it from turning dark brown. Then cover the apple with salt (non-iodized is best). Set it aside to dry for several weeks, turning it occasionally. Your apple-head will shrink and shrivel into a wrinkled old face!

After three or four weeks, clean off your creation and spray it with clear varnish. Decorate the character by gluing on yarn or cotton-ball hair. Try using rice kernels or corn for teeth. Use your imagination! Poke cloves or round-headed pins in the eye sockets, or glue beads in for the eyes. You might even make a body of a wire coat-hanger armature dressed with doll clothes you've stuffed with rags.

Your amazing apple-person may "thrill you to the core!"

Teacher's Tip

- Early settlers in North America made dolls for their children using materials they found, such as: straw, wood, corn cobs, and corn husks. The Iroquois Indians made figures (perhaps for sacred rituals) with dried apples for heads.

Clay Food Creations

- Advanced Gourmet
- Best Finished Later

<u>Trompe l'oeil</u> literally means "to deceive the eye." Ceramic artists Richard Shaw and Marilyn Levine have created leather items, books, and much more from clay. These items look so realistic that they trick the viewer.

Try a realistic-looking ceramic item yourself—one of your favorite foods in clay: a hot dog, slice of pizza, taco, bacon and eggs, pie, or whatever your favorite food may be!

FIRST, look at magazine pictures (or better yet, the real thing) and decide how to copy the textures and forms of the food you wish to make. There are 3 basic methods of working by hand with clay: pinching it, coiling it into "ropes" of clay, and flattening it into slabs.

Try using clay tools or wooden sticks.

THEN, when you're done, your piece must be allowed to dry. If your fun food has been made of fire clay, it must be "baked" (fired) in a special oven called a kiln.

NEXT, the work can be finished with glazes and then fired again, or it can be painted with acrylics. If you paint your piece, mix life-like colors to copy the real thing.

Are you tempted to try a ceramic sandwich or a clay cupcake? This idea really does "take the cake." Just don't munch this lunch or you'll break a tooth!

List of Lessons by Art Media

Acrylics .... pages 28, 29, 46, 48, 55, 73

Ceramic Clay .... page 75

Colored Chalks .... pages 15, 28, 39

Drawing Tools .... pages 27–29, 31, 33, 37–39, 53, 60, 61, 70

Fibers .... pages 14, 21, 72–74

Glue .... pages 23, 27–29, 36, 46, 50, 51, 54, 59, 62, 64, 65, 67–69, 74

Oil Pastels .... pages 28, 33, 37, 47

Papers .... pages 12, 13, 15, 17, 21, 23, 27, 28, 31, 33, 37, 39, 43, 46–51, 53, 60, 62, 64, 70, 73

Tempera .... pages 47, 48, 54, 55, 58, 59, 73

Watercolors .... pages 23, 58, 65, 70, 72

GLOSSARY

Aesthetics - artistic, well-chosen; the science of the beautiful

Abstract - subject-matter simplified to its basics until it is unrealistic

Acrylics - quick-drying synthetic paints, water-based

Assemblage - an additive form of sculpture constructed by arranging and joining pieces together

Background - that part of the picture plane which seems to be farthest from the viewer

Balance - a principle of design; equable visual forces in a work of art

Batik - a method of decorating fabric using resist materials and dyes

Blending - mixing smoothly and gradually

Brayer - rubber roller with a handle, used to apply printing ink to a surface

Byzantine - an artistic style, usually with a religious theme, which developed around Constantinople (as it was known then); it consisted of a rich blend of Greek, Roman, and Asian styles

Center of interest - focal point; that to which the eye is attracted

Ceramics - the art of making clay products

Cohesive - holding together; unified

Collage - pasting various materials together to form a work of art; usually two-dimensional

Colorant - pigment, dye, paint, stain

Composition - the way the elements of an artwork are organized

Continuous line - the uninterrupted mark of a moving point

Contour - outline, boundary

Contrast - showing a noticeable difference when compared side by side

Craftsmanship - mastery, skill, finesse

Crosshatching - technique using crisscrossing lines for shading

Design - arrangement of the elements in a work of art

Drybrush - using a paintbrush with most of the moisture removed from the paint or ink

Embellish - to adorn and decorate

Enhance - improve, enrich, elaborate

Firing - tempering with heat, as with pottery

Fixative - usually a spray, it helps to make permanent such media as charcoal and pastels

Form - a shape that takes up space; an object with three dimensions

Freehand - to sketch without the aid of a pattern or instruments with which to measure

Geodesic - pertaining to the use of math to measure curvature

Glaze - (noun) a glass-like coating; or, (verb) the act of applying a vitreous coating, as on pottery

Hatching - using a series of fine parallel lines to shade when drawing

Highlight - spot of highest value in a drawing or painting; the opposite of shadows

Horizon line - where the sky seems to meet the earth or the sea

Idiom - an expression, a saying, jargon

Intensity - brightness or dullness of a color

Intermediate colors - also called Tertiaries; those colors made by mixing a primary color with a related secondary color: red-orange, red-violet, blue-violet, blue-green, yellow-green, yellow-orange

Kiln - furnace in which clay pieces are hardened by firing

Knead - to mix by working with the hands

Line - mark drawn with a moving tool; the path of a dot through space

Medium - an art material; plural form is media

Mosaic - a design made by inlaying pieces of different colors, traditionally marble, glass or tile

Motif - theme or subject used repeatedly

Negative space - the background within which a design is placed

Non-objective - having no recognizable subject or objects

Opaque - that quality that does not allow light to pass through; the opposite of transparent

Overlapping - arranged with overlying edges; partly covering

Papier-mâché - French for "chewed paper;" an excellent medium for strong, lightweight sculptures

Parallel - corresponding; arranged in the same direction

Pastels - chalky pigments held together with a substance and molded into stick form; also a synonym for pale or light-colored

Pictorial - representational; a likeness

Polymer medium - a thinning or finishing material used in acrylic painting, often glossy

Pop art - early 1960's American style featuring popular culture (mass media, comic strips, and advertising)

Portrait - image of a person; often the face and upper body

Primary colors - the principal colors of red, yellow, and blue, from which all other colors are made

Printmaking - technique in which an image is transferred from one surface to another

Profile - side view; usually of a face

Realistic - true to nature and fact

Recede - to move back

Relief - where patterns and forms project above a flat background surface

Render - to express, interpret, create

Resist - (noun) a material that withstands; or, (verb) to strive against

Sculpture - a three-dimensional work of art, usually made of wood, stone, metal, or clay

Secondary colors - orange, green, and violet; made by mixing two primaries together

Senses - the five physical faculties: sight, taste, touch, hearing, and smell

Shading - the use of light and shadow to create the impression of depth

Shape - a closed line; an outlined area; a two-dimensional area

Sketch - quick drawing

Stabile - a three-dimensional design in space without motion

Stencil - a means of applying a cut-out pattern to a surface

Still life - inanimate, non-moving objects

Stippling - using small dots to gain an effect, often shading

Subject - an image that can be identified in a work of art

Support - that which backs up, sustains, and bears the weight of art materials

Symbolism - using an image to stand for or represent something else

Tactile - refers to the sense of touch

Technique - skill or method of performance

Tempera - water-based pigment such as school poster paint

Tertiaries - (see Intermediate colors)

Texture - that element of art which refers to how things feel to the touch, or how they look as if they might feel

Tint - a higher value of a color; made by mixing that color with white; the opposite of shade

Tone - (verb) to bring to a desired shade or color

Tortillon - a rolled-paper blending stump

Transparent - see-through, clear

Trompe l'oeil - French for "deceive the eye;" creating the illusion of reality

Underglaze - special color painted on a ceramic piece before the glaze is applied

Unity - wholeness, undividedness

Utilitarian - useful

Value - lightness or darkness of a color

Vertical - straight up and down; at right angles to the bottom edge of the paper; parallel to the side of the paper

Wash - a thin coat of watery color

"I always wanted to write a book
that ended with the word 'mayonnaise.'"

Richard Brautigan

mayonnaise